Arles

Guidebook

Museums
Monuments
Excursions/Tours

COORDINATION
Odile Caylux

PREFACE
Christian Lacroix

INTRODUCTION
Jean-Maurice Rouquette

TRANSLATED FROM THE FRENCH BY
Charles Penwarden and John Tittensor

VILLE D'ARLES

onum, Éditions du patrimoine

Contributors

ALDO BASTIÉ
Historian

MICHEL BAUDAT
Art historian

CLAUDE BERTIN
Art historian

MICHÈLE BERTIN
Art historian

PATRICK BLANC
Mosaic restorer, Musée de l'Arles Antique

ODILE CAYLUX
Heritage Officer, City of Arles

ALAIN CHARRON
Curator, Musée de l'Arles Antique and Musée Réattu

ÉRIC COULET
Director, Camargue Nature Reserve

GILLES DESSOMME
Mission chief, Domaine de La Palissade

VANESSA EGGERT
Art historian

JULIEN FAURE
Mission chief, Musée Camarguais

ANDREAS HARTMANN-VIRNICH
Lecturer, Université de Provence

MARC HEIJMANS
Archaeologist, Musée de l'Arles Antique

JEAN-LOUP LEREBOURS
Director, Médiathèque d'Arles

ALINE MARTIN
Head of Development, Arles Office of Tourism

ANNE MATHERON
Administrator, Abbaye de Montmajour

JEAN-LOUIS MOURGUES
History teacher

MICHÈLE MOUTASHAR
Head Curator, Musée Réattu

LYDIE PASTRE
Arles Tourist Office

SYLVIE REBUTTINI
Librarian in charge of the City Archives

PHILIPPE RIGAUD
Historian

JEAN-MAURICE ROUQUETTE
Honorary Head Curator of the Museums of Arles

BOUZID SABEG
Director of the Heritage Department of the City of Arles

DOMINIQUE SERENA
Director, Museon Arlaten

MARIE-HÉLÈNE SIBILLE
Curator, Musée Camarguais

CLAUDE SINTES
Head Curator, Musée de l'Arles Antique

CATHERINE SOUSSOUY
Landscape designer

ISBN 2-85822-650-4

“What belongs to Arles belongs to me”, since Arles belongs to us all!

Our heritage takes shape and abides in the place where we are born, where we learn to walk and where we live. In Arles my eyes are master of all they survey, from the unmistakable texture of its soft stone to the silhouettes of its streets, the facades of its houses, the gaze of its windows. “I hear” Arles: the sound of trains borne on the mistral wind, the sharp crack of a sudden squall, words heard here and nowhere else, noises and murmurs from the Lices, the sound and the fury of the arena, the chiming of the hours. But Arles can be touched, too: its rugged parapets, smooth marble, cool ironwork. And it can be breathed –the air of the sea and the Camargue hovering over the Rhône, fig trees in the summer heat, the damp of its mysterious palaces– and endlessly, pleasurably “tasted”, from garlic through to aniseed. Its heritage is all this, but it is, too, the enduringly special character of the rebellious, excessive, demanding, indolent, discreet, eccentric people who live among Arles’ old stones; it is the work they do, and the city’s history and the history of all these families handed down as local sagas and tales of cultural mixes. Arles is in the eye of all the winds, ground zero for the meeting of East and West, of northern and southern, intersection of river and sea, of roads from Rome and the road to Spain, of innumerable beliefs and influences. All of which means Arles will never give in to the temptation of the pitiful, everlasting peace that afflicts “museum cities”. Wary as it may be, Arles is paradoxically exposed –I might even say “condemned”– to modernity, irretrievably caught up in art and the immediate, and in the special intensity they take on here as if at an epicentre of political, social and religious complexities.
There’s something of the Phoenix arising from its ashes, or a new Penelope, in this ancient necropolis whose buried treasures endlessly transmute into contemporary energy. Music and books being published, all the world’s languages being spoken, people learning to turn sunlight into photos... This is how a heritage is made fruitful, by this recycling of earlier strata, of the vivid patchwork that draws deep into its weave all the life-giving forces of the near and the distant past, all those twentieth century exiles or nomads just passing

Lee Miller Dressed as an Arlesian, *Picasso, 1937 (Musée Réattu).*

through. Arles is at once working-class and imperial, rustic and aristocratic, Christian and pagan, modest and proud, classical and traditional, stark and baroque, austere and unbridled. Apollo and Dionysus. In colour and black and white. I made these paradoxes my own, growing up "stone by stone", feeding off the contrasts that in turn have become the substance of my work: bullfighters in suits of light and shadowy old people wearing mourning, dreamwork from the Théâtre Antique and ordinary everyday chaos, gilt cribs at Christmas and street-wisdom in summer, caravan Gypsies and touches of local elegance, ancient Venuses and Picasso odalisques, Delacroix Algerians and Raspal's eighteenth-century Arlésiennes, museum paintings and photos from the Rencontres, southern patois and cosmopolitan visitors, tradition with Frédéric Mistral and avant-gardism with Van Gogh (I wonder did they ever cross paths on the Place du Forum!), Provençal opulence and Camargue aridity, the ancient and the contemporary. I would not exist without this "philosopher's stone" heritage, this alchemy of so many sensations hoarded then spent. What I see, I keep; but I grow because I give in return. The key here is not so much the idea of an eloquent past as that of a present whose voice is always there in the background. It's a question of belonging and communication: heritage is a state, a kind of store we dip into as consumers of ourselves and of what surrounds us. Part of humanity's heritage, we offer ourselves in return, like the man who never budges from where he is, but journeys inside those who do.

CHRISTIAN LACROIX

Contents

History of Arles

Guidebook

■ From the Place de la République to the cryptoportiques

The World Heritage tour

■ From the Place Voltaire to the Espace Van Gogh

The Ramparts tour

From the Place Lamartine to the Place du Forum

The Rhône tour

From the Museon Arlaten to the Musée de l'Arles Antique

The Vieux-Bourg tour

Around Arles...

History

of Arles

Preceding pages: the banks of the Rhône, Arles.

• • • The beginnings

Arles, dazzling halo for a modest limestone hill rising out of the marshy plain of the Rhône delta. Only 25 metres above sea level, this is a city born of a friendly conspiracy with its river. Here at the gateway to the Camargue was the perfect site for a bridge, for a river port offering ready access to and from the sea. A unique location –the intersection of the coast road to Spain and a busy river leading north into the heart of Gaul– that was to be the key to the city's growth and prosperity in Roman times.

In Neolithic times the nearby Alpilles were the heartland of the highly developed civilisation that left us the famous hypogea, or underground chambers, at Fontvieille; yet Arles itself has yet to yield the slightest trace of any prehistoric past. On the other hand, the Greeks come from Phocaea to found Marseille in 600 BC had been quick to realise the economic significance of the Rhône valley and to make contact with the native Ligurians living in their oppida, defensive positions of drystone walls set up at various vantage points.

While it is not easy to know exactly what form the relationship took –was early Arles a colony of Marseille or just a trading post?– precious information is to be found in Festus Avienus' *Ora maritima,* in which the Latin poet draws on ancient sources: "There stands the city of Arelate, called Théliné in olden times, when the Greeks lived there." Thus it would seem that "nourishing" Théliné, the creator of wealth, had preceded the political emergence of a native city with the Celtic-sounding name of Arelate, "the city near the marshes".

Scale model of the Forum (Musée de l'Arles Antique).

Scale model of the Roman city (Musée de l'Arles Antique).

The archaeological excavations of the last few decades have gradually brought this distant past to light. Of the twenty or so sites concerned, that of the former Winter Garden offers the most impressive evidence of a changing scene as, from the middle of the sixth century BC up until approximately 400 BC, river traffic from Marseille brought ceramics –dishes from the eastern Mediterranean, amphoras from Marseille– in steadily increasing quantities.

The early fifth century BC saw the first signs of a city in the Hellenistic style, a city whose brick and adobe buildings on their drystone foundations were carefully laid out to form an urban grid.

Their rooms looked onto an enormous central courtyard with direct access to the street, the total built-up area covering more than thirty hectares.

Towards the middle of the fourth century BC, a clear political shift began to make itself felt in the new city of Arelate, with the indigenous culture coming more into its own: local pottery became the rule, while land division practices and the creation of rooms and outbuildings for such specific purposes as domestic use and handicrafts reveal more intricate social organisation. In the first half of the second century BC, well before Rome's large-scale military operations against the Salluvii in 125 BC, Italian merchants enjoyed steadily increasing influence within the remarkably prosperous Arlesian economy. We later learn from Julius Caesar that

Fragment of an attic goblet (6th century BC), found in 1976 during the excavations in the Jardin d'Hiver.

Roman mosaics in the Musée de l'Arles Antique

The earliest reference to the discovery of a mosaic in Arles dates from 1574, but it was only in 1831, at the instigation of Honoré Clair, that fragments of a "common" mosaic were actually collected.
A municipal council document of 1851 states that the lifting of two mosaics had recently been "effected with the utmost precaution" by an expert from Lyon, but the works in question are known to us only through watercolours by François Huard. Hippolyte Bazin's Guide du Touriste Archéologue (1896) mentions yet another mosaic, but it was 1901 before a pavement was actually lifted and restored. Since 1995 the Musée de l'Arles Antique and its restoration unit have been responsible for the preservation of other pavements as they come to light.
SO FAR about a hundred of the mosaics created in the Arelate of the first to the fourth centuries have been identified. Although many of them have not survived the passage of time, the pavements held by the Museum are of a quality and thematic diversity that makes the collection one of the richest in France. Many of them come from the Trinquetaille district on the right bank of the Rhône, where enormous villas had been built

during the difficult siege of Marseille, which had espoused the cause of his enemy Pompey, he resorted to the Trinquetaille shipyards for the building, in a single month, of the dozen warships he urgently needed.

• • • The Roman colony

An exceptional strategic position, a solid economy and a population that had made the right choices during the civil wars: these were the factors that led Julius Caesar to choose Arles for Rome's first colony in the lower Rhône valley. Suetonius has graphically recounted the mission of Tiberius Claudius Nero, father of the future emperor Tiberius: in September 46 BC, he and the veterans of the Sixth Legion founded a Roman-law colony on an immense territory in part confiscated from the people of Marseille; under the reign of Augustus the new settlement would be named *Colonia Julia Paterna Arelate Sextanorum.*

THE AUGUSTAN CITY – The earthworks involved in its transformation into a colony radically altered the physical structure of the pre-Roman town, making it virtually unrecognisable and dividing it up into a straight-line grid that at once determined the siting of the major public monuments. Still a perceptible presence in the street network of modern Arles, the grid may not actually have extended to the entire city, which at the time covered no more than forty hectares. A wall –prestigious symbol of a Roman colony– defined the urban area as such. The road from Italy brought visitors into the town via a monumental gate protected by two round half-towers: this is now called the Porte d'Auguste ("Gate of Augustus").
From 40 BC onwards a massive town planning programme got under way. In addition to the building of the city walls, it focused on the creation of enormous public spaces –attested to by the early esplanade discovered under the paving to the south of the Forum and the pedestal decorated with mouldings under the *Hôtel d'Arlatan*– and included the city's first three major building projects: the Forum, the Théâtre Antique and the Arc du Rhône. The most striking feature of this initial venture is the sheer consistency of an architectural programme in which the Forum, in the lower part of the town, complements and sets off the Théâtre Antique above the acropolis, while the Arc du Rhône provides a powerfully symbolic point of entry. This unity of design signals an ideological concept worked out to the last detail at the highest government level.

Mosaic (Musée de l'Arles Antique).

ARLES UNDER THE FLAVIANS AND ANTONINES – The rapid economic growth and resultant urban expansion that marked the end of the first century BC saw the town break out beyond its early boundaries. Except on the eastern edge of the hill, where they were retained, the Augustan city walls were abandoned in favour of the creation of new neighbourhoods. This change was particularly marked to the north where, in the last ten years of the century, large-scale excavation paved the way for the building of an impressive amphitheatre half-way up the hill.

The alignment of the theatre generated a new urban pattern, running at a tangent to the earlier grid and leading to the pontoon bridge in the bend of the Rhône, where the current was at its weakest. This second planning venture extended to the right bank of the river and today's Trinquetaille district.

Trinquetaille too had been colonised during the Augustan period and developed rapidly as the local shipyards and industrial sites began to concentrate upstream. Downriver, not far from the port facilities along the bank, luxurious villas began to spring up, their marble or mosaic-floored rooms arranged around a peristyle. This was the beginning of the residential role the district was to retain down the centuries to come.

Similar changes were taking place on the south side of the city, where the levelling of the ramparts had made room for a tradesmen's quarter; however this was soon pushed further out, to be replaced by such splendid residences as the two villas on the site beneath the present Crédit Agricole bank; dat-

behind the port facilities of the time. Recent excavations have brought to light several new examples in the southern part of the old city, in the Winter Garden, on the Esplanade des Lices and under the Crédit Agricole bank. Almost all of them were part of patrician residences. In contrast with other floors of opus siginum (cement sometimes decorated with multicoloured stones) and opus sectile (sheets of marble arranged in geometrical patterns), the mosaics offer a rich geometrical and narrative repertoire, with their frequent allusions to the loves of Jupiter (*The Rape of Europa, Leda and the Swan*) and the tales of the gods and heroes (*Dionysus drunk, Hercules and the Hydra of Lerna, Jason and Medea, The Medusa*). With his hand resting on the zodiac, Annus-Aion, the god of time, appears in two mosaics from Trinquetaille, while the presence of the seasons in four pavements testifies to the importance set on fertility and the golden age by the wealthy Romans of Arles.

The use of certain geometrical compositions, set patterns and florets reveals the influence of the workshops at Vienne, further north, but also that of African mosaicists: further proof, if any were needed, of Arles' key role as a port. P.B.

ing from the last quarter of the second century AD, they were decorated with remarkable mosaics. The most impressive example of urban development, however, was the building of an enormous racecourse 400 to 450 metres long, 101 metres wide and with room for twenty thousand spectators. Because of its size it had to be built outside the city proper.

By the end of the Early Empire, then, Arles had all the marks of a major city. It possessed a superb central area –forum, theatre, amphitheatre, circus, temples, triumphal arches and porticoes– and highly efficient public services including an aqueduct bringing water to both banks of the Rhône, a sanitation system, a bridge across the river, shipyards, a port and industrial districts. The city was literally walled in, except for the part of its eastern side given over to a vast necropolis and luxurious residential suburbs. Thus the city's shipping and trading activities combined with the area's natural wealth to underpin a phase of prosperity and large-scale investment lasting almost two centuries.

And yet the period around 260 AD saw Arles deep in crisis. A series of fires caused considerable damage to property in the town, certain districts were sinking into poverty and others were abandoned outright by their inhabitants. Although these problems were not necessarily simultaneous, they are symptomatic of a period of pronounced insecurity that doubtless reflected the political turmoil Gaul was going through at the time.

• • • The Christian city

And yet its inherent economic dynamism enabled Arles to come through the crisis and make the most of Diocletian's refounding of the Empire. Two symbolic events mark this renaissance: firstly, in 313 the mint was transferred to Arles, where the striking of gold and silver coins was to continue until the fall of the Roman Empire. And secondly, in the following year the Emperor Constantine called a Council there, attended by representatives of forty-four Western Churches. While it is true that merely occasional visits by a sovereign hardly sufficed to give Arles the status of a true capital, there was a real official awareness of its strategic importance: as a vital staging post for communications between the Empire and a Western Europe overrun by the barbarians, the Rhône delta was later to become Rome's ultimate bastion.

For the time being at least, Arles' newfound prosperity was sufficient to allow for a fresh programme of urban improvements. In the heart of the city an enormous area right on the banks of the river became home to a splendid public baths which tradition has named the Thermes de Constantin (Baths of Constantine). Opposite the baths, the early portico with its nine single-storey shops was replaced by a groin-vaulted walk leading to the square. The core of this impressive architectural composition was a monumental entry mounted on its own purpose-built base and providing access to the Forum from the square lower down. The remains of this four-columned porch have since been incorporated into a facade on the Place du Forum, where they can still be seen today. Constantine's reign was also to bring major changes to the circus, where the *spina* –the wall dividing the actual arena down the middle– was partly demolished, refaced with marble and topped with the obelisk that was to find a new home in front of the town hall in the seventeenth century.

The obelisk, Place de la République.

In contrast with many of the cities in Roman Gaul, urban development in Arles was to continue right through the fifth century, both in the civil sphere and in that of church architecture. One of the most substantial projects was the raising of a new city wall, which was to prove a stepping stone between the initial Augustan rampart and Arles' medieval fortifications. A relatively summary assemblage of enormous blocks of stone, this wall was slightly shorter than its predecessor and enclosed the main monuments –the south portico of the theatre and the south exedra of the Forum– before gaining the bank of the river via what is now the Rue Jouvène. A second major project, to the south of the baths, was an elaborate rectangular building 57 metres long and 21 metres wide, whose remains can be seen inside the *Hôtel Arlatan;* this was the civil equivalent of a basilica, a meeting hall and venue for public audiences with high-ranking political personalities. Its construction probably coincided with the transfer to Arles, in the early fifth century, of the prefecture of the Pretorium of the Gauls.

A signal event in the life of the city, the arrival of the prefect of the Pretorium of the Gauls and his numerous staff was soon to be followed by the Emperor Honorius' decision to call a meeting of delegates of the Council of the Seven Provinces in Arles every year between 13 August and 13 September. A rescript of 17 April 418 has the following to say: "The city is so fortunately located, business so brisk and traders so numerous that all the products of the universe are brought together there... Arles is the place the Mediterranean and the Rhône seem to have chosen to marry their waters and create a meeting point for the nations living on their coasts and shores." Thus it was that Arles became the administrative and political capital of what remained of Roman Gaul.

At the same time major military operations were taking place. After gaining supremacy in Gaul, the usurper Flavius Claudius Constantinus had chosen Arles as his capital, with a view to controlling the road to Italy. Initially recognised by Honorius under the title of Constantine III, he was later besieged in his capital by the patrician Constans and, in spite of having been ordained a priest, decapitated. These events, which led to Arles' becoming a regional and provincial capital, were also to leave their mark on the city's religious history: it was inevitable that the bishop of a city of this standing should entertain hopes of rising to the rank of primate within the Church hierarchy.

The Arles trades seal, 15th century.

The Christian community in Arles was one of the most ancient in Gaul. It is known that the city had a bishop since 254 and its first martyr, Genesius, in approximately 250. The Council of 314 had been a feather in its cap, but real prestige came with a letter of 22 March 417 in which Pope Zosimus granted Patroclus, Bishop of Arles, the rank of metropolitan –archbishop– for the whole of the former Narbonne diocese, together with the right to provide letters of recommendation to all members of the clergy, including bishops, wishing to go to Rome. Challenged by other bishops, these privileges were to be the source of many conflicts. In the mid-fifth century Pope Leo the Great was on the point of sharing out responsibility between the Churches of Arles and Vienne, further north, but the onslaught of the Barbarians threw the ecclesiastical administrative system into chaos and ultimately reinforced Arles' supremacy. In 513 Caesarius, Bishop of Arles, was entrusted by Pope Symmachus with the supervision of Church affairs in Gaul and given authority to convoke councils. From the relatively large number of texts that have come down to us from this golden age of the Church in Arles, we can deduce that today's archaeological record is only a meagre indication of the extent of ecclesiastical building at this period.

The first group of episcopal buildings dates from the fourth century and was situated in the southeastern part of the walled city, near the Tour des Mourgues. A life of St Honoratus, Archbishop of Arles, written c. 430 makes mention of the cathedral, but also of a funerary basilica in which he was buried. This is doubtless a reference to the church of St Genesius at Les Alyscamps, renamed Saint-Honorat in the Middle Ages. An account of the death of St Hilary of Arles

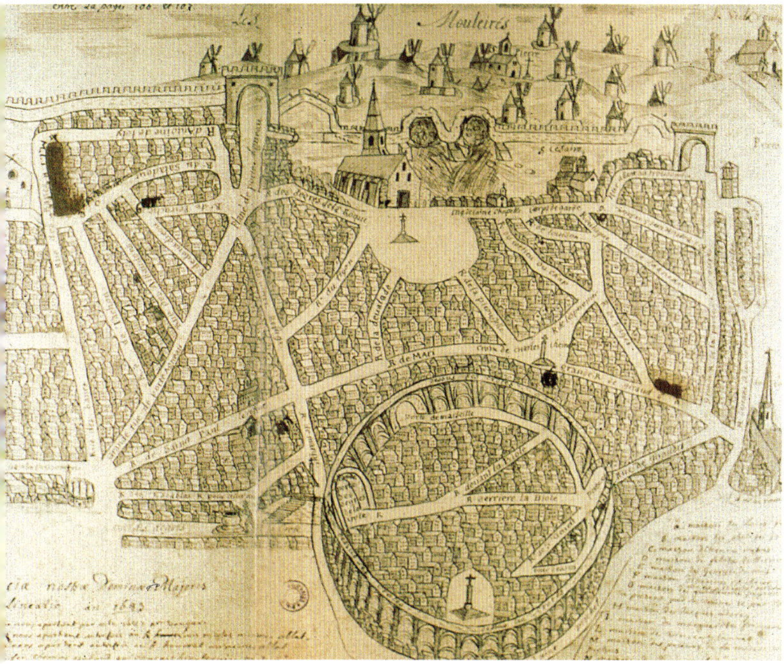

The L'Hauture district (drawing, 17th century).

in 449 states that the body was displayed in a basilica dedicated to St Stephen, the first Christian martyr. Thus the cathedral seems to have been transferred by this time to the centre of the city, where it continued to be called Saint-Étienne (St Stephen) until its dedication to St Trophimus in the twelfth century.

CAESARIUS, BISHOP AND SAINT (502-542): The fearlessness of his faith, his doctrinal rigour and a pastoral zeal well served by his exceptional eloquence made Caesarius the leading ecclesiastical figure of his time. Born in Chalon-sur-Saône c. 470, this Burgundian came from a Catholic family with Gallo-Roman roots. At eighteen he took the tonsure, the first step towards holy orders, and entered the service of his bishop; two years later, however, he decided to withdraw from the world, opting for the monastery at Lérins. There he remained for ten years, acquiring a sound education but endangering his health with excessive self-mortification. Sent to Arles for treatment, he met the orator Julius Africanus and was ordained by Bishop Aeonus, who then made him abbot of the monastery. He was to be chosen as Aeonus' successor in 502, a large part of his forty years as bishop being marked by political and religious strife due to the invasion of the Arians. **Famed as a preacher** – he has left us 238 sermons covering all aspects of Christian life –Caesarius was also a theologian

Authenticated document, Priory of Malta, 15th century.

and lawmaker concerned to ensure the written recording of tradition while guiding the many Church councils he supervised towards decisions favouring the parishes and the training of the clergy. A monk at heart, he made the monastic ideal the root of his work. At the time only a single monastery for women existed in all of Gaul, in Marseille. It was there that he sent his sister Caesaria, before putting her in charge of the enclosed-order community he founded in 512 in Arles' L'Hauture quarter.

• • • Arles under the Franks

Their triumphal entry into the city in 536 earned the Frankish troops a warm welcome from the people of Arles, who saw their arrival as bringing peace and renewed religious unity to Gaul after decades of Arian dominance. However Arles, like the rest of Provence, was to find itself enmeshed in fratricidal conflicts between the Merovingians and later the prey of fresh invaders. War broke out between Sigebert and Gontran in 570, with one of the latter's expeditions having dire consequences for Provence. In 585 the Visigoths diverted the Rhône and flooded Arles, which had already suffered an incursion by the Lombards in 573. Between 541 and 767 the city fell victim to at least ten outbreaks of plague, not to mention the periodic ravages of dysentery and smallpox.

After a brief respite during the reigns of Charlemagne and his son, the second half of the ninth century brought new disasters. Disembarking in the Camargue, the Normans pillaged Arles in 859, but the major threat was now the Saracens. Already masters of Spain, they wasted no time in reaching the Rhône in 721, sparking on the Frankish side a riposte so vigorous that it did as much damage to the area as the initial invasion. After his victory over the Saracens at Poitiers, Charles Martel, grandson of Charlemagne, led a campaign in the South of France that left the region devastated, yet even this failed to prevent the Moors from coming back up the Rhône and pillaging Arles in 842 –and again in 850. A final invasion and plundering took place in 883.

The city suffered dreadfully from this succession of events. By the mid-sixth century all its outlying districts were abandoned and the population had fallen back around the original hill, inside a hastily reconstructed city wall. By this time the great monuments of old –the arena and the theatre– were being used by the Arlesians as defensive shelters, the city being reduced to the role of a citadel, a last refuge for the people of a ravaged region.

Arles' role as a political and administrative capital changed considerably during the tribulations of the Frankish period. For the first time the decision-making centre had left the Mediterranean for northern Gaul, with Frankish Provence governed by a nobleman living in Marseille. It was not until the Carolingian period that a count took up residence in Arles, but he was to remain a relatively insignificant figure until the founding of the Kingdom of Provence, also known as the Kingdom of Arles. The king, Louis the Blind, was an invalid who lived shut away in Vienne and finally handed control to his cousin Hugh of Arles, so called because he lived in the city from 911 to 926 before becoming king of Italy. The truth was that power was gradually slipping away from these kings, to be seized by the now hereditary counts

View of Arles (drawing, 17th century).

and their families. The expulsion of the Saracens, in which the king played no active part, was to provide these nobles with a chance to fulfil their ambitions.

In 883 a troop of Saracens settled at Le Freinet, overlooking Saint-Tropez, in the place now known as the Massif des Maures. From this base they launched an ever more daring series of raids all over the Alps. When in 972 they captured Maïeul, the Abbot of Cluny and demanded an enormous ransom, the outcome was a veritable crusade which saw Guillaume, Count of Arles and Roubaud, his brother, drive out the Saracens once and for all. In addition to the resultant prestige, "Guillaume the Liberator" was granted the title of marquis and an appropriate quantity of land. Thus it was that the Counts of Arles, now also Marquises of Provence, came to establish the first independent dynasty, with Arles as their capital and Montmajour Abbey as their place of burial.

These were difficult times for the Arles Church, too. While St Caesarius' successors still possessed all sorts of papal privileges, their authority began to decline in the seventh century and the absence of a list of bishops for the period 683-788 is a sure sign that written culture had lost considerable ground. By contrast there was a marked upswing in the Carolingian period, when archbishops joined members of the aristocracy at all the major religious and political assemblies. There was even a regional Church Council –the only one, as it happened– in Arles in 813. From the tenth century onwards the bishop's chair in Arles was filled by members of the leading families, all from Burgundy and all using their family connections with the counts to increase their power. Manassès (920-961) is a typical example: son of a Count of Chalon and nephew of Hugh of Arles, he had links with all the local aristocracy and the chapter was filled with his relations: Gontard, the provost, was the brother of Teucinde, founder of Montmajour Abbey, which she was to exchange with Manassès. Gontard was also Bishop of Fréjus, a title that would later pass on to his nephew Riculfe... Now the bishops swore loyalty not to the king but to their archbishop!

• • • The medieval renaissance

Apart from consolidation of the power of the new dynasty founded by the counts, the main outcome of the expulsion of the Saracens and the new sense of security it brought was an economic revival accompanied by a marked population increase. There began a period of urban growth that saw the city once more spill out beyond its fortifications as its new peripheral districts took shape.

In 972 houses began to be built outside the walls, near the downstream church of Saint-Laurent. In 1015 other residences appeared south of the ramparts, beyond the Porte Saint-Étienne. The first half of the twelfth century saw the rise of the Le Bourg district –now known as La Roquette– comprising houses, a communal bread oven, flour mills, two churches (Sainte-Croix and Saint-Laurent) and a ferry over the Rhône. The land belonged to the Porcelets family, whose fortress and Chapelle Saint-Maurice stood on what is now the Place Antonelle. By the close of the century Le Bourg had acquired its own rampart and become a separate urban entity, heir to the core of the old Roman colony and a religious and political centre with its own cathedral and numerous churches.

The link between Le Bourg and the city itself was Le Méjan, an area whose ownership had often been the subject of armed conflict. It was here that the Trinitarian monks, in search of unoccupied land, set up their monastery in 1203. But already Le Bourg had become Le Vieux-Bourg (the "Old Town"), urban sprawl having extended north to Le Trébon, around the castle belonging to the Les Baux family. With its hospital, two churches (Saint-Julien and Saint-Isidore) and nearby Le Marché (today's Porte-Agnel district), Bourg-Neuf –the "New Town" and now the La Cavalerie quarter– was also enclosed by an extension of the ramparts. Towards the south another new quarter based around Notre-Dame-de-Beaulieu, one of the fifteen parishes, sprang up between the Porte Saint-Étienne and the fringes of Les Alyscamps. On the right bank of the Rhône the village of Trinquetaille –a fief of the Count des Baux with its houses grouped around the church of Saint-Pierre and a number of convents– also had its own wall.

With a population of some 15,000, Arles was now Provence's second-largest city after Marseille. It was also the most spectacularly fast-developing in the closing years of the twelfth century, with its built-up area having doubled –from 18 to 36 hectares– in only two hundred years.

The Arles Black Book of Privileges, 15th century.

THE GREGORIAN REFORMATION – While Guillaume the Liberator was busy consolidating his title and landholdings in the late tenth century, a few important families from the same circles were helping themselves to large chunks of public and, especially, Church property. They it was who would take over the bishoprics and colonise the chapters.

This concentration of wealth and power was highly significant. In Arles three strong-minded, long-lived prelates of venerable lineage had the entire eleventh century to themselves. Such was the power of the Archbishop of Arles that he was the ecclesiastical equal of the feudal count. It is symbolic, too, that the city itself was divided between the two camps by a neat horizon-

Facing page:
detail of the principal door, Saint-Trophime cathedral.

tal line, with the Count to the north, the Archbishop to the south –and the lion's share going to the latter!

Times change, however. Inspired by the Abbey of Cluny and with the support of the monastic orders, the reforming current within the Church was to succeed, with the election of Pope Gregory VII (1073-1085), in proscribing the choosing of bishops by the nobility and thus in cutting the direct connection between the civil authorities and the episcopacy. Yet it took many years of struggle for Gregorian prelates to gain their independence via free elections, press for the monastic life for their canons and rebuild the temporal power of a Church fragmented by lay intrusion.

This newly regained prosperity allowed the chapter to undertake the rebuilding of Saint-Trophime, create a cloister and other monastery buildings, and inspire and carry through an impressive architectural programme in Arles and its eight parishes. Hundreds of different projects now put into practice the "antique" style so dear to medieval Provençal art. However, this very wealth and the clergy's fierceness in reclaiming their rights quickly generated hostile reactions which were to give the movement for emancipation of the city a violently anticlerical character.

THE "REPUBLIC OF ARLES" – In addition to the great landholding families outside the city –the Les Baux at Bourg-Neuf and Trinquetaille, the Viscounts of Marseille at Le Marché, the Porcelets and later the Les Baux at Vieux-Bourg– Arles was home to families of urban knights who, as well as owning vast tracts of land, had custody of the fortresses surrounding the major Roman ruins. The trade revival and the income accruing from their lands meant substantial fortunes, and these gave them a mounting role in the life of the city. The consulate they founded in 1131 was among the first in Provence and was granted a charter by the archbishop in 1150.

Twelve in number, the consuls sat for a single one-year term after being coopted from a council of 120 members, half of whom were knights and *probi homines* ("honourable men"). Thus the knights and a few wealthy families made up Arles' patriciate, which dominated a highly aristocratic consulate in which the middle classes and the common people played no part.

Until the early thirteenth century the consulate was controlled by the archbishops. In 1207 a hardening of positions emerged between the patriciate and the middle classes as the Count of Provence sought to re-establish his former role in local political life. From 1220 to 1235 tension was running so high that the city had to be administered by a Podesta, a professional politician employed for a year; Arlesians were not eligible for this post and as a general rule the Podesta was an Italian.

The period 1235-1251 saw the appearance of the *Confratria des Baiuli* ("Brotherhood of the Farmhands"), whose aim was freedom from the authority of the great landowners. However the body had a markedly aristocratic and anticlerical character, the movement it represented being closely associated with the Cathar heresy. The archbishop's palace was put to the sack, Church property seized and civil marriage encouraged. The Brotherhood's power lasted from September 1235 to July 1238, but the organisation ultimately succeeded in besting neither the Church nor the other social classes. The then archbishop Jean Baussan appealed for help to the Count of Provence, granted him control of the city and admitted a provost to Arles as the representative of the Count's authority.

The accession of Charles of Anjou, brother of St Louis, to the countship was the signal for further strife that included renewed anticlericalism, occupation of the archbishop's palace and the massacre of the Hospitallers at Trinquetaille. Driven from the city, Archbishop Baussan once more appealed to the Count, this time offering in return his entire jurisdiction. On 30 April 1251 the Count's army entered Arles, which was thus to go the way of all the other cities of Provence: never again would it be independent.

• • • Angevin Arles

In 1245 the sudden death of Raymond Berenger V, last of the Catalan counts, saw Provence pass to his fourth daughter Béatrix, wife of Charles of Anjou. One of the new sovereign's first acts was to abolish the consulate, the symbol of Arles' political independence. The Count was to be represented at Arles by a provost, a judge and a treasurer, who would exercise power without reference to elected municipal representatives. The only concession to the City was the right to name four trustees who would take charge of administration. The trustees had to be housed and the City settled for the rental, then the purchase of a simple house near Saint-Trophime; the Count, by contrast, was proprietor of the renovated *Palatium,* buildings that had formerly been the palace of the Podesta. There the provost lived, the judge handed down his decisions, the treasurer collected the Count's revenues and prisoners languished in the dungeons that can still be seen today. The inhabitants held their general assemblies on the square to the north, now known as the Plan de la Cour. Royal officials were sworn in on the stone terraces still visible in front of the facade.

On the other hand the Arlesians were granted certain privileges by the Count which they busily set about extending once the civil war and the fact of Louis II's minority began working in favour of increased autonomy for France's cities. However the royal officials ceaselessly flouted the charters they had sworn to uphold and the result was ongoing tension and mistrust on the part of the Arlesians.

The people had prevailed on the Count to give up his plans for a keep in the city. Thus Arles was not to be a royal residence, in contrast with Tarascon where Louis II had set about building the superb "castle of King René" in 1400. Fearing increased royal intervention, the residents had limited the official presence to ten constables. The Arlesians endlessly vaunted their city's unique status as "land adjacent" to the Count's domain, but the provost's residence in Provence's largest municipality was a mere empty shell. Arles was capital of itself and no more, a besieged city in the middle of a deserted region. Little by little its charters, rights and privileges were emptied of their content.

This explains the gradual abandonment of the city by its Angevin sovereigns. Worst of all, however, was the fact that this political decline took place in a period of great adversity. Like Provence's other cities, Arles suffered the full impact of the classic misfortunes of the late Middle Ages: famine, plague and war.

Drawings from the Treatise of Surveying by Bertran Boysset, Arles surveyor and chronicler, late 14th – early 15th century.

Despite the fertility of the surrounding countryside, the city knew many periods of famine caused by bad harvests and war. Most terrible of all, however, was the bubonic plague, which swept the area in 1348 and remained endemic for many years. In addition, the second half of the fourteenth century saw these scourges exacerbated by the miseries of war and the havoc wrought by roving bands of looters.

The human toll occasioned by this succession of disasters was heavy indeed. In a single century Arles lost half of its population. The countryside was ravaged and entire villages –Saint-Martin, Vaquières-en-Crau, Trinquetaille, Albaron and Le Castellet, near Montmajour– wiped out. The outlying working-class districts were in ruins and the monks from monasteries outside the walls took refuge in the city. The population slide had been as hard on the clergy as on the faithful: so little remained of the religious communities that three parishes had to be abolished. Nonetheless religious fervour continued to run high. And while it was rare that the archbishops should actually live in Arles –they often held high office at the papal court in Avignon– open expression of popular attachment to the Church was in no way diminished. One indication is the extraordinary success of the "Montmajour Day of Atonement", a pilgrimage held on 3 May in veneration of the relics of the True Cross held in the abbey. The Arles chronicler Bertran Boysset (c. 1345-1415) has it that the 1409 pilgrimage drew no fewer than 150,000 of the faithful! Similar enthusiasm was shown in 1448 when, on the orders of King René, Jean d'Arlatan supervised the exhumation of the relics of the "Three Saint Marys" under the church of Notre-Dame-de-la-Mer –just at the time when the Gypsies were arriving in Provence.

• • • French Arles

On 11 December 1481 Charles III, Count of Provence, died in Marseille, designating Louis XI as his heir. Addressing the Provençal parliament on 15 January 1482, Palamède de Forbin, Louis' representative, committed himself to maintaining the identity of the Count's domain within the king-

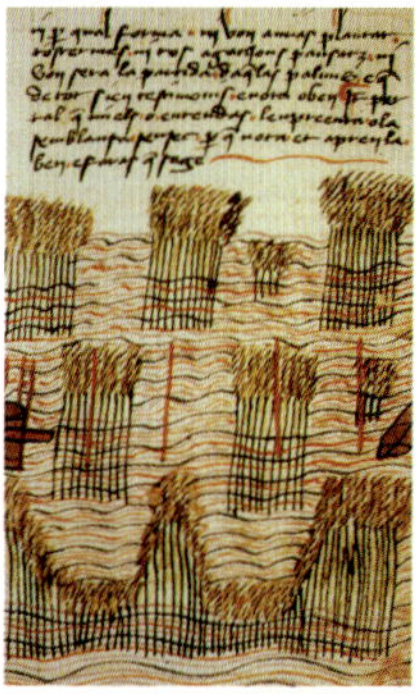

Above and facing page: drawings from the Treatise of Surveying *by Bertran Boysset, Arles surveyor and chronicler, late 14th – early 15th century.*

Late medieval houses in Arles

The remains of medieval houses in Arles are not immediately apparent to the untutored eye. Yet if we take the trouble to consult the manuscripts of the time we can readily conjure up an image of everyday life in Arles during the Middle Ages.

THE HOUSES of Arles were mainly built of stone from the quarries at nearby Fontvieille and Beaucaire, with frequent use of dressed stone for the facades. It is possible that more modest dwellings were made of wood or adobe, but if so none of them have survived. As a rule houses were two-storey, the few exceptions –those with three storeys– belonging to the especially rich; access to the upper levels was by a straight or spiral staircase. The townhouses of the fifteenth and sixteenth centuries sometimes enclosed their spiral staircase in a polygonal tower, the staircase thus giving onto galleries surrounding an interior courtyard and providing access to the rooms.

WATER CAME from wells situated either in public places or in the courtyards between houses. Only the very rich could offer themselves the luxury of a sink, water pipes and toilet. Fireplaces with chimneys were similarly restricted to the privileged classes, the poor having to make do with hearthstones for heating and cooking purposes. Similarly, only the well-to-do could afford doors and windows decorated in the taste of the time, together with the murals and painted ceilings that are the most visible remains of a now somewhat neglected architectural style. V.E.

Autem ovna · danar · qiar fai
ti sera do ner · q s'si faic s lo contrari
p q nota · o ben · e fai ne q s fage

dom, to respecting its legal institutions and to preserving its charters and privileges. Further, as a sop to the vanity of the Arlesians, he re-established the title of Consul, lost along with the "Republic" in 1251. Having then bought the landholdings of Trinquetaille from the archbishop, the Consuls acquired –and retained until the revolution– the resounding title of "consuls, governors, lieutenants-general of police and lords of Trinquetaille". In 1592 each of them received from the City two long red robes, one of velvet for winter and the other of damask for summer!

Its geographical situation had made Provence an important element in France's military operations during the Italian wars, but the other side of the coin was its vulnerability to attack by the Holy Roman Emperor's Imperials. At the time of the invasion of 1536, Charles the Fifth, after having himself crowned King of Arles in Aix-en-Provence, laid siege to the city. However his imperial army, decimated by dysentery, harassed by the local peasantry and short of food in an area devastated by scorched-earth tactics, soon withdrew. The Arlesians remained convinced that the decisive factor in this victory had been the two rounds of cannon-shot fired by Monsieur Porcelet from the Tour des Mourgues as the Imperial vanguard advanced from Saint-Pierre-de-Mouleyrès!

For Arles the moment of danger had been acute but brief. Much more serious were the chaos and terror the Wars of Religion were to generate over the next half-century. Arles itself saw only two major outbreaks of violence, around 1561-62, when the war was at its very gates (the battle of Saint-Gilles, the sack of Beaucaire and Les Baux) and especially between 1588 and 1594, when the city was rent by the Catholic League civil war, fomented by the sinister Lieutenant Biord. Unsurprisingly, for Arles the entire period of the Wars of Religion was one of deep insecurity.

Natural disasters were a further complicating factor. "Unseasonal weather fluctuations" saw periods of drought alternating with floods and gruelling cold snaps: in 1510 wolves had

The lion of Arles

The lion is a significant feature of the iconography of the great door of the Saint-Trophime cathedral and the possibility of a link with the lion on the city's coat of arms cannot be discounted.
AT THE TIME of the Consulate the lion also appeared on the city's heraldic devices, one example being the treaty signed between Arles and Marseille in 1215 and now held in the archives of the City of Marseille. Suspended from the parchment is a seal showing on one side a part of the Arles ramparts and on the other a lion and the motto *Nobilis in primis dia sol et ira leonis*. Was there also a link between the lion and the procession organised by the City every year on St Mark's day, 25 April? Lack of evidence means that for the time being we can do no more than speculate, but it is a matter of historical fact that a lion was given as a gift to the City by the Count of Provence; details of the cost of its food are to be found in the municipal account books. In the mid-sixteenth century, however, the City found the heraldic animal's upkeep costly and pointless and decided to dispose of it. L.S.

come as far as the Crau plain and in 1570 the olive trees around Arles froze and died.

As in the previous century there were recurrent outbreaks of plague, especially in 1580 when even the conduct of the war was affected. Nonetheless, the incorporation of Provence into the Kingdom of France continued.

Royal visits to Arles were always greeted by enthusiastic displays of loyalty, notably in January 1516, when François I was acclaimed after his victory at Marignan and again in 1533, when he was en route for Marseille for the wedding of Henri the Dauphin and the young Catherine de Médicis. The king's authority, already manifested in the founding of the Parliament at Aix-en-Provence in 1501, was underscored by the choice of archbishops. What the see of Arles lacked in terms of income it easily made up for in prestige and its conferment was a highly political affair, rewarding displays of loyalty or services rendered. Scion of an illustrious Genoese family, Cardinal Nicolas Cibo (1489-1499) was the first of a long line of foreign archbishops, his successors –the Ferriers, uncle and nephew– being Spanish. Highly cultured men and generous patrons, they were responsible for the introduction of Renaissance art to Arles and were much involved in organising resistance to the Reformation when it began to infiltrate the diocese. In the twenty years following 1550, however, the unpredictability of royal policy led to the appointing of prelates for whom Arles was simply a pay-off or a mere step up the career ladder.

In spite of its difficulties, Arles took advantage of the periods of peace to rebuild its economy, the crucial factors here being marked population growth and the arrival of migrants from Italy and elsewhere in Provence. Given the overall circumstances this prosperity was somewhat surprising, but it was to make a real contribution to the local flowering of the Renaissance.

By the second half of the fifteenth century their retreat inside the city walls had forced a number of religious communities to build new churches. These communities included the Preaching Friars, who between 1448 and 1499 built the superb basilica of Notre-Dame-de-Confort in the Flamboyant Gothic style and the Cordeliers, who settled for a splendid bell-tower. The death of Cardinal Aleman in 1450 triggered massive pilgrimages to his tomb and led the Saint-Trophime chapter, between 1454 and 1475, to replace its Romanesque choir with an enormous apse and ambulatory. The majestic elegance of this structure makes it one of the masterpieces of the Flamboyant revival in Provence. While still little felt in the field of religious architecture, this fresh

Facing page: the lion of Arles in the Arles Black Book of Privileges, 15th century.

Below: the Arles coat of arms.

creative urge was to bring radical change in the form of substantial residences set around a central area lined with walks. **The Hôtel** de Laval-Castellane and the Saint-Thomas and Sainte-Luce commanderies of the Knights of Malta –all taken over from the Knights Templars– are superb examples of the arcaded central courtyard combined with deliberate recourse to monumental proportions. Long, admirably decorated facades broken up by horizontal dripstones marry an old Gothic military style, all merlons and false machicolations, to enormous Renaissance bays adorned with sumptuous mouldings. In some cases the façades include rectangular or diamond-shaped blocks or staircase turrets combining a Flamboyant gable with medallions, all signs of the prestige then enjoyed by Italian decorative styles.

Arles in the 17th century
Engraving by Peyret, 1660.

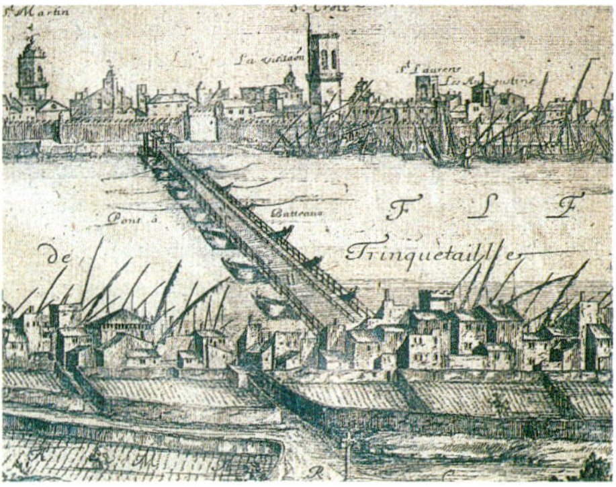

However, the city's familiarity with its ancient architectural heritage was to give its new buildings a specifically local feel. The past was back in force, from the simple recycling of old materials in the Hôtel des Amazones to the diabolically skilful copies of friezes from the Théâtre Antique used for the facade of the Hôtel de Donines. The century was marked above all by two magnificent buildings: the Hôtel-Dieu hospital, begun in 1573 and its chapel in the Rue du Lau; and even more so the town hall belfry, built between 1543 and 1558 and modelled on the Mausolée des Jules in Saint-Rémy-de-Provence.

• • • Arles in the 17th century

The reign of Henri IV opened the way to a long period of peace and prosperity, during which the city was fortunately spared the turmoil of the Fronde. Twice kings of France sojourned in Arles, Louis XIII in October 1622 and Louis XIV in January 1660. These were truly sumptuous occasions, the royal itinerary being marked out with triumphal arches bedecked with emblems and heraldic devices that left a vivid impression on the popular imagination. The undulating mouldings still to be seen under certain windows are nothing other than stone renderings of the precious draperies hung out to welcome Louis XIII.

Until this time the area of the city had changed little, its 54 hectares a mass of tiny plots squeezed inside the thirteenth-century walls. Except for the Jesuits, who had taken over the ruins of the Théâtre Antique, religious and charitable bodies found themselves obliged to set up outside the walls, with a diadem of churches and gardens taking shape along the southern face of the city.

Stripped of all political and administrative possibilities –by now Aix had taken over as capital of Provence– Arles' prestige depended solely on its function as an episcopal see. The seventeenth century was a time of great religious fervour there, with the new spiritual momentum due to the Council of Trent being exploited by a succession of remarkable archbishops including the Arles-born Gaspard du Laurens (1603-1630), a model prelate and –for once– a prophet recognised in his own country. Never in the course of the century had the city drawn so many new religious orders: the Minims, Oratorians, Ursulines, Jesuits, Carmelites, Visitationists, Augustinians, the Sisters of Our Lady of Charity of the Refuge, the Sisters of Mercy and the Discalced Carmelites. Each order had to add its own church to the dozen already built by the older orders, the four confraternities of penitents and the three commanderies of the Knights of Malta. With the population on the rise, the religious revival also found expression in the renovation of the parish churches. Although four of them had been closed, there were still eight in the city in 1700, five of which –Saint-Pierre, Sainte-Anne, Saint-Martin, Saint-Julien and Saint-Laurent– had recently been rebuilt or extended in the Late Gothic style; and at century's end Monsignor de Grignan endeavoured to introduce contemporary architecture into his cathedral. When the Angelus rang out from Arles' forty or so churches and chapels, nobody could pretend not to hear it!

Arles in the 18th century.

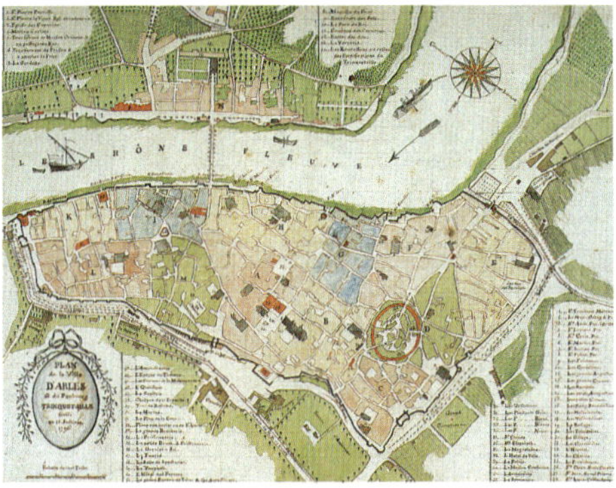

The Grand Prieuré, now the Musée Réattu.

Labouring under the crushing debts incurred during the Wars of Religion, the City had had to cede large parts of its domains to its creditors, which in turn had led to the creation of enormous private estates. Scattered along the Rhône

Pierre Véran: Hand-drawn map of Arles in 1803 (Arles Media Library).

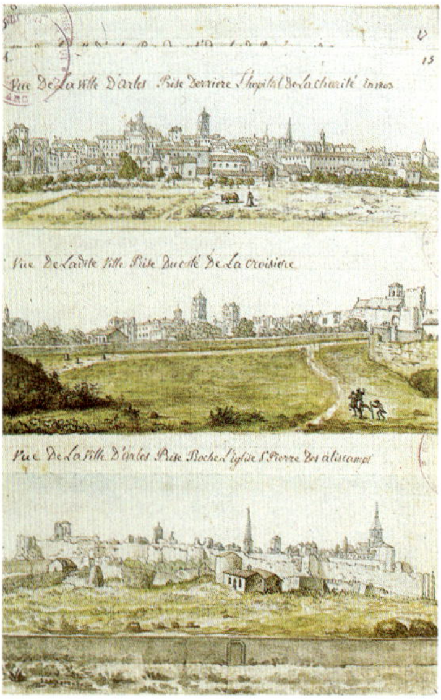

downstream, from 1600 onwards this succession of holdings was to play a part in the reclamation of the Camargue, left unfarmed for decades. Under a two-yearly rotation system of wheat growing and sheep raising this fresh, fertile ground was to be the basis of the fortunes made by Arlesian landowners. The slow but steady growth in farm income over an entire century saw a proliferation of townhouse building by these aristocrats and bourgeois, until a full tenth of the city area was taken up by them. The paradox, of course, was that all this rural wealth was in the hands of city-dwellers: with the exception of L'Armellière, the splendid residence raised by Pierre de Sabatier in 1605, there was not a single château in the Camargue!

At the same time the city was a permanent building site. In addition to all the places of worship being built or rebuilt and the hundred or so great houses undergoing constant improvements, the Consuls were busily improving Arles' public spaces and "making the streets more pleasant and more convenient". In 1679 an overall alignment of the city's facades was decided on.

Virgin and Child in the Genoese style, church of Saint-Pierre de Trinquetaille.

The century's uncontested architectural masterpiece was the new town hall, a symbol of the city's enduring grandeur set in its very heart, between the Romanesque palace once occupied by the Podesta and the Renaissance clocktower. This complex project took ten years, finally being concluded in 1676 by the Paris architect Jacques Peytret, assisted by Jules Hardouin-Mansart. The Consuls then decided on a tribute to Louis XIV, re-erecting on the Place Royale the obelisk recovered from the ruins of the Roman circus and crowning it with a gilt-bronze sun. Thus the city reflected the glory of its king!

A further indication of the intellectual ferment of the time was the creation in 1666 of one of the first provincial academies. Its founders, eight young belles lettres enthusiasts, modelled their new institution on the Académie Française.

However, the turn of the century was to see this momentum broken by a period of crisis. First came the tragic winter of 1709, when the crops were destroyed and the olive trees killed by frost; there followed floods, famine, imposition of an intolerable tax burden and, finally, the Great Plague of 1720, which cost Arles 10,000 of its 27,000 inhabitants. The city was left a shadow of its former self and while prosperity returned relatively quickly, the time of the great building projects was over.

Arles' families now began to worry more about improving their personal living environment than trying to impress others with ever more elaborate houses. This was the golden age of Arles cabinet making, with local craftsmen turning out handsomely worked white walnut furniture of great refinement and elegance. At the same period the women of Arles adopted a distinctive style of dress, designed both to draw attention to their charms and assert their identity. Thus attired, they were to become a favourite subject of Antoine Raspal (1738-1811), the most naively sensitive painter of his generation as well as its most sublime illustrator.

Jacques Réattu, The Triumph of Liberty, *1794, (Musée Réattu).*

• • • The French Revolution in Arles

A further disastrous winter in 1789 again reduced to poverty a population enraged by the refusal of the privileged classes to accept the principle of equal taxation. March saw the political debates preliminary to the election of France's Estates General taking place against a background of rioting caused by food shortages and the high price of wheat. Rising against their parliamentary representatives, the Arlesians took over the city. On 4 August the Consuls were stripped of their powers, which were entrusted to a council of 8 noblemen, 5 members of the clergy, 14 representatives of the middle classes, 16 merchants and craftsmen, 5 peasant farmers and 1 fisherman. In spite of everything the oligarchy lived on!

Increasing popular discontent then led to the triumph of the "patriots" in the municipal elections. On 15 February 1790, with the backing of the local craftsmen and sailors, Pierre-Antoine d'Antonelle was elected first mayor of Arles. On 13 January 1791, in the collegiate church, he inaugurated

Pierre-Antoine d'Antonelle, first mayor of Arles

Born in 1747 in the La Roquette district of the city, Pierre-Antoine d'Antonelle was baptised in the Eglise Sainte-Croix. Members of the gentry, his parents had married in 1745 and already had a son, Jacques-Philippe. Pierre-Antoine was not to know his father, who died a few months after his birth. Raised by his mother for a military career, he reached the rank of lieutenant and was incorporated into his regiment in 1762. Military life did not suit him, however and in Paris he led a profligate existence before resigning from the army in 1782 and returning to Arles. He was forty when the French Revolution broke out and as a great admirer of Voltaire held advanced, anticlerical ideas that clashed with his social background. Elected mayor in 1790, he became a member –and secretary– of France's Legislative Assembly in 1791. In 1792 he was almost elected mayor of Paris. President of the Jacobins Club and then of the jury at the trial of Marie-Antoinette, he was considered an "anarchist"; several times in political difficulty under the Directory and the Empire, he finally rallied to the Restoration cause. On his death in 1817, only pressure from the then mayor of Arles, Perrin de Jonquières, induced the local clergy to give him a church funeral. O.C.

the Society of Friends of the Constitution, open only to "true patriots".

At a time when the issue of the conforming clergy was a source of deep social division, this act of exclusion and d'Antonelle's aggressively anticlerical stance provoked a rapid riposte. On 4 June 1791 the city's "honest citizens" decided to take over the Society, which they renamed the Society of Friends of Peace and Order. The National Guard was reorganised and non-juring priests readmitted.

Meeting in the house of Canon Giffon, the honest citizens became "Chiffonists", wearing a silver siphon as their insignia and recruiting their members in the L'Hauture and La Cavalerie districts. The other camp was that of the "Monnaidiers", named after the La Monnaie quarter at La Roquette, where they met in the Augustinian church. Their emblem was a coin. The resultant rivalry between L'Hauture and La Roquette was to remain a feature of life in Arles until the First World War.

Violence was henceforth an everyday affair. Driven out of the city, the Monnaidiers took refuge in the Camargue while the Chiffonists, victors in the November 1791 elections, gradually turned Arles into a royalist stronghold. On 21 March 1792 Arles was officially declared in a state of rebellion and a thousand-strong army from Marseille, complete with cannons, set out across the Crau plain. On 27 March it entered the city without a shot being fired, Arles' 5000 Chiffonists having fled during the night.

Thus the Monnaidiers returned to power, but the overall situation showed little improvement: the people of Arles were hungry, the flight of the Chiffonists had left widespread unemployment in its wake and the City had to cover the costs of the army that had been raised to put down the counter-revolution. In April 1792 a new club was formed in the Église des Pénitents-Blancs at La Roquette and backed with a "Committee of Sabres" designed to strike terror into the hearts of the Chiffonists. September saw a number of unofficial executions, but for the rest –the men having fled– vengeance was exacted from the women, who were forced to ride through the city seated backwards on donkeys.

After a brief Federalist outbreak in July 1793, during which the Monnaidiers found themselves exiled, the Revolution began to take its course again: the churches were closed, Saint-Trophime became the Temple of Reason, the Place du Forum was dedicated to Marat, the obelisk was topped with a "Phrygian" liberty cap and all public buildings, including the town hall, were stripped of the trappings of the Ancien Régime. Little by little, however, the moderates began to find these mea-

View of Arles, early 19th century.

sures intolerable and after the events of 27 July 1794 the extremists lost control of the city. On 15 February 1795 the club was closed and its surveillance committee dissolved. The municipality was once again in the hands of the Chiffonists and the Monnaidiers were outlawed in a seesawing of power that was to continue throughout the period of the Directory (1795-1799) in line with the political crises in the capital.

Under Napoleon state dependence consolidated the role of the former Chiffonist leaders, several of whom went on to extremely successful careers. The Concordat of 1801 brought religious peace, but it also sealed Arles'fate as an episcopal city and thus reduced its political influence even further.

With the fall of the Empire in 1815 the Republicans found themselves faced with the White Terror. Once again they had to flee, hiding –as did all local fugitives– in the marshlands of Plan-du-Bourg and the Camargue.

• • • The contemporary city

The taste for ruins that was so much a part of the Romantic spirit was not slow to come to Arles. In the late eighteenth century the friars of the mendicant order of Minims set about collecting the sarcophagi spread around Les Alyscamps and using them to line the avenue leading to the Église Saint-Honorat, reflecting the prevalent notion of a Roman necropolis. This charmingly naive arrangement was accompanied by commendable efforts to rescue other relics of the ancient past and display them in the suitably dignified context of the roofless nave of their church. Under the terms of an agreement signed with the Consuls on 7 December 1784, the nave officially became the first "Public Museum of Antiquities", open daily to all.

In 1825, under Charles X, Arles mayor Laugier de Chartrouse undertook the clearance of the amphitheatre, then occupied by 212 houses and 2 chapels. The restored site was inaugurated in 1830 with a bullfight that drew 20,000 enthusiastic spectators.

In 1823 similar enthusiasm had initially greeted the plan to excavate the ruins of the Théâtre Antique, whose visible part was by then reduced to two columns belonging to the stage and a handful of arcades where the portico had been. Being less energetically pursued, however, the project only bore fruit seventy-five years later, part of the explanation being that the business instincts of the local bourgeoisie prevailed over the romantic urge to breathe new life into the past. The official cult of progress meant a blind advance to which not even the most historically significant sites were immune, and by the middle of the century Arles had entered a new era and irrevocably broken with its past.

On Sunday 9 July 1848, the inaugural steam train bearing 600 official travellers drew up in the Arles railway yards at

Provençal bullfight in the Arles arena.

11.06, after pulling out of Marseille at 8.30. The opening of the Lyon-Marseille line was to transform life in the city. The building of the railway yards and the locomotive shed in the centre of Les Alyscamps had wiped out one of the handsomest burial grounds of all Antiquity and the triumph of the railway signed the death warrant of Arles' river traffic. While the train journey took only a few hours, the convoys of barges up the Rhône took twenty-eight days –and thirty when the mistral wind was blowing!

The abrupt end to inland waterway transport was a mortal blow to the Arles economy and the 4000 people –a quarter of the population– who made a living from the river. To reduce the resultant unemployment the P.L.M. (Paris-Lyon-Mediterranean) rail company chose Arles as the site for its workshops, which by the end of the century were providing jobs for up to 1800 people. And so Arles, which hitherto had lived off its lands and its river, was gradually evolving into the industrial centre of which the Barriol shipyards and the Étienne Paper Mills, founded in 1882 and 1911 respectively, would be the backbone. At the same time the farming population –still some 40 per cent of the Arles total in 1850– had left to settle the surrounding countryside. The face of the city had changed beyond recognition.

As a result of a rapid rise in the urban population, a strikingly anarchic collection of working-class neighbourhoods had sprung up outside the walls. The first of these "suburbs" took shape beside the railway line on the slopes of the Colline de Mouleyrès, previously home to some twenty windmills. This was a warmly working-class area –its population was largely made up of railwaymen– whose revolutionary place names celebrate a total absence of town planning. More recent and

On the Rhône.

overtly bourgeois in character, the Chabourlet neighbourhood to the south of the city was made up of neatly aligned detached houses mingling comfort and pretentiousness.

On the outskirts and in the city proper, roads had long been a major concern of the city fathers. The late eighteenth century had seen the opening-up of today's Boulevard Émile-Combes, while at La Roquette the present Boulevard Clemenceau already extended from the Tour de l'Écorchoir to the Porte du Marché-Neuf. Rebuilt in the triumphal style in 1706, this latter gateway was demolished in the name of progress in 1876. In the course of the 1820s the Boulevard des Lices was extended through the gardens of the former Carmelite convent, and with the opening of the iron bridge in 1875 it provided direct access to Marseille and Languedoc. Ten years later the Rue Gambetta, even though its completion was a laborious affair lasting from 1883 to 1896, was already the city's main artery.

The second half of the nineteenth century also saw the disappearance of the city wall. The houses immediately inside were, so to speak, "turned around" and their new outward-looking facades complemented at ground-floor level with a long line of cafes whose terraces were protected from the sun with canvas awnings. Thus was born an urban setting based on a lifestyle characteristic of southern French towns and their emphasis on the pleasures of conviviality.

By contrast, the old central area clung to its traditional appearance, give or take a few obvious changes. The damage

Arles market.

caused by the Revolution had been considerable, with several churches destroyed and many others having undergone the ordeal of heedless secular use. Abandoned by the families who had built them, the townhouses had fallen into ruin or been bought by shopkeepers who ripped out their facades. The turn of the century brought two luxurious new establishments to the Place du Forum, in the form of the *Hôtel Nord-Pinus* and the *Hôtel du Forum*. It was on the Place du Forum, too, that Frédéric Mistral, the great Provençal poet, unveiled his own statue on 30 May 1909. The sun the Arlesians were so fond of began to become a magnet for foreign visitors as well: in search of Classical Antiquity, drawn by the famed beauty of the city's women, fascinated by the work and the memory of Van Gogh (a resident from February 1888 to May 1889) or quite simply passing through on their way to the coast, more and more travellers paused to discover Arles and the Camargue. And ever since, tourism has been one of the pillars of the local economy.

The Second World War hit Arles hard. Bombed five times between 25 June and 15 August 1944, the city lost its station, its two bridges, almost a third of its houses, and the churches of Saint-Julien and Saint-Pierre. In addition, the amphitheatre, ramparts and Notre-Dame-de-la-Major suffered heavy damage.

Women of Arles in traditional costume.

Detail of traditional headwear.

Appointed to oversee the work of reconstruction, architect Pierre Vago opted for a new church at Trinquetaille that would include the magnificent stained glass work of Alfred Manesser (1954). After decades of vacillation the building of a new hospital, to replace the 1573 Hôtel-Dieu, was entrusted to Paul Nelson; the result was France's first health complex, completed in 1974 on the Colline de Fourchon. In 1995 came the opening of the Musée de l'Arles Antique, designed by Henri Ciriani and built near the remains of the Roman circus. This imposing triangular structure now houses all the City's collections of antiquities, an archaeological research institute and information facilities for the public. Thus three major buildings have given contemporary architecture a natural place within a heritage going back further than most. Arlesians, though, have long been aware of the virtues of this kind of symbiosis; after all, since the beginning of the nineteenth century the major historical sites have enjoyed a new lease of life –in Orange as well as in Arles– as venues for what have now become distinguished large-scale festivals. And for over thirty years Arles' Rencontres Internationales de la Photographie has been consolidating its reputation as one of the world's leading photography events. Not many places in the world can bring together thousands of people every July and sit them before a giant screen in a Roman theatre as they savour the mildness of the Provençal night.

Guidebook
Arles

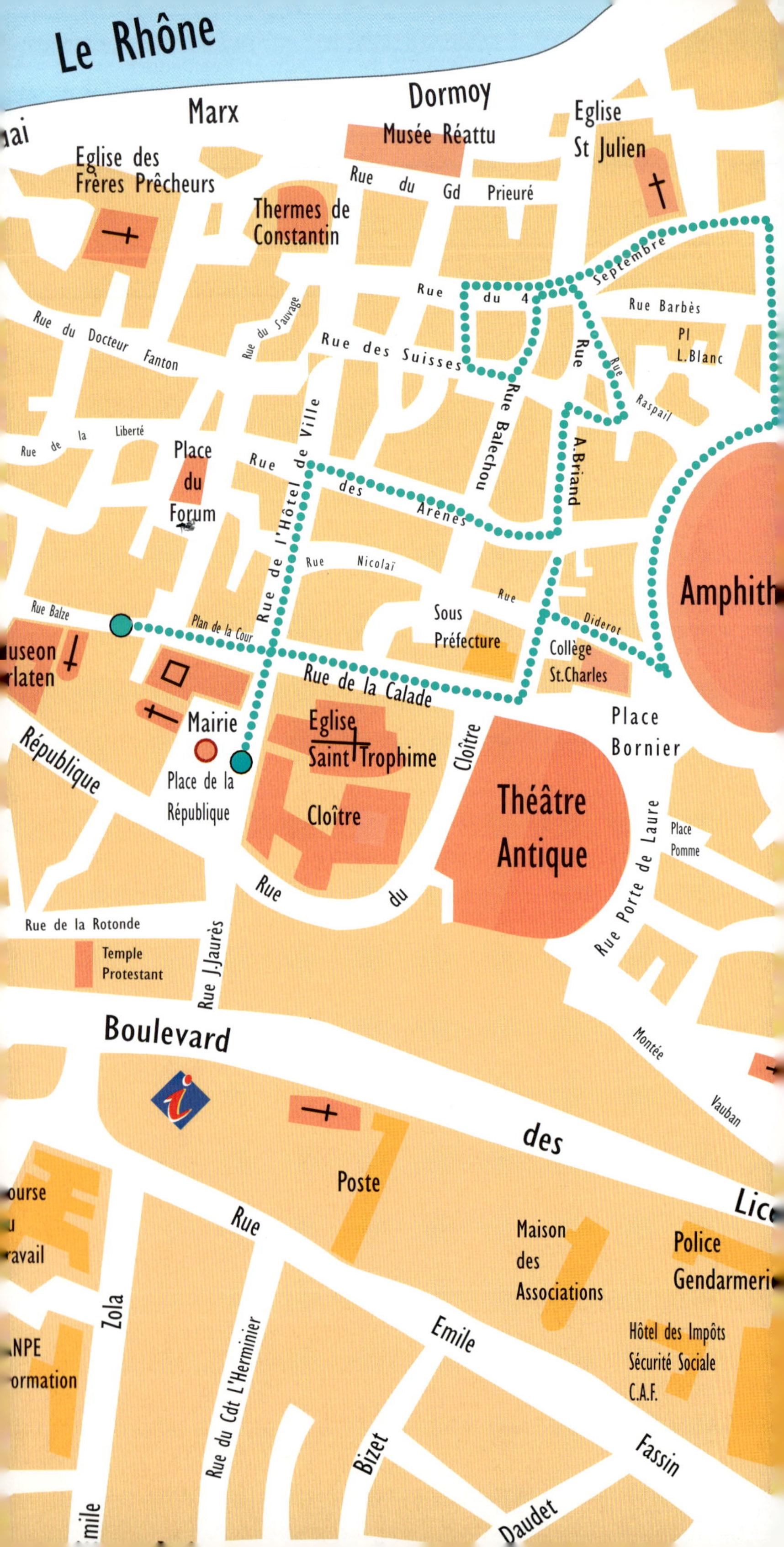

Le Rhône
Marx
Dormoy
Musée Réattu
Eglise
St Julien
Eglise des
Frères Prêcheurs
Rue du Gd Prieuré
Thermes de
Constantin
Rue du 4 Septembre
Rue Barbès
Pl
L.Blanc
Rue du Docteur Fanton
Rue du Sauvage
Rue des Suisses
Rue Balechou
Rue Raspail
Rue A.Briand
Rue de la Liberté
Place
du
Forum
Rue des Arènes
Rue de l'Hôtel de Ville
Rue Nicolaï
Amphith
Rue Balze
Plan de la Cour
Sous
Préfecture
Rue Diderot
Collège
St.Charles
Rue de la Calade
Mairie
Eglise
Saint Trophime
Place
Bornier
République
Place de la
République
Cloître
Théâtre
Antique
Place
Pomme
Rue du Cloître
Rue Porte de Laure
Rue de la Rotonde
Temple
Protestant
Rue J.Jaurès
Boulevard des Lic
Montée Vauban
Poste
Rue Emile Fassin
Maison
des
Associations
Police
Gendarmeri
Hôtel des Impôts
Sécurité Sociale
C.A.F.
Zola
Rue du Cdt L'Herminier
Bizet
Daudet

From the Place de la République to the cryptoportiques

The World Heritage tour

1. Detail of sculpture, cloister of Saint-Trophime.
2. Cloister of Saint-Trophime.
3. The Hôtel de Ville.
4. Model of the amphitheatre.

This itinerary offers a view of the outstanding monuments for which Arles was made a UNESCO World Heritage site in 1986. These are essentially Roman and Romanesque. Walking in central Arles, which is now a conservation area, we can still get an idea of how the Roman colony was laid out. Subsequent building in this area followed the grid pattern established at this time. Consequently, whatever the historical changes of style, Arles' architectural heritage is notable for the spirit of continuity linking its monumental and urban ensembles, from the Roman forum to the bishop's palace and the imposing classical town hall.

Place de la République

THE HEART OF TODAY'S TOWN, the Place de la République is sited on what was once the southern end of the Roman forum. The eastern side was occupied by the episcopal city, which grew continuously between the Middle Ages and the Revolution. In fact, before successive developments brought it to its present size, the square was originally just a narrow forecourt outside the primatial church of Saint-Trophime. The houses on the north side were destroyed in the fifteenth century. The seventeenth century was decisive for the square's development. This, for example, was when the famous obelisk was erected. Also, the facade of the church of Sainte-Anne was moved back in the 1620s and, fifty years later, the town hall was built around an old clocktower left from an earlier building. However, work continued. In the eighteenth century, the townhouses on the southern side were destroyed. In 1810, the old medieval gate (Porte de Saint-Étienne) beside the Bishop's palace (Palais de l'Archevêché) was demolished. In 1857, the newly laid Rue Jean-Jaurès afforded direct access to the Boulevard des Lices, giving the square the appearance we know today, with its stylistically diverse facades. This rectangular perimeter lined by Saint-Trophime, the Bishop's palace, the town hall and the church of Sainte-Anne resembles an Italian piazza. O.C.

Saint-Trophime Cathedral

Place de la République

Relief on the portal.

Little us known about the predecessors of today's cathedral. It is thought that the original see was located in the southeastern corner of the Roman walls and was transferred to its current position near the forum around the beginning of the fifth century.

UNDER THE WESTERN BAY of the nave are a series of vaulted chambers from late antiquity, running between two parallel walls pointing in north-south direction, alongside the old *cardo*, or main thoroughfare, which went past the medieval church. The edifice was built on the same site and used the ancient walls as a substruction for the facade and southern, gutter-bearing wall. Remains of mosaic flooring found under the second bay tend to indicate that the Romanesque church was built over a structure already existing on the site. In fact, it is likely that the earlier building stood slightly further to the east, beyond the first bay.

Inside the church

The church, one of the finest Romanesque buildings in Provence, was built in several phases, in the course of which the original plan was changed. Visitors entering through the sumptuous western facade will, so to speak, be going back in time as they head towards the transept, this being the oldest part of the building (a Flamboyant Gothic choir replaced the apses of the Romanesque chevet in the third quarter of the fifteenth century). While plans to build a new cathedral were probably made earlier in the eleventh century, work could not begin until some time around 1100. This started with the chevet and the transept, which were built using a course of medium-to-large stones. The plans were ambitious. In the arms of the

transept, the arches of the crossing and the blind arches of the west wall support arcading on the upper level, a kind of false blind triforium which was surmounted by a level of openings below the original vault. This vault was later lowered. The crossing of the transept is surmounted by a dome supported by squinches. The drum communicates with the surrounding spaces through four round openings. It was made in rag-stone, no doubt hidden by a form of cladding or decoration. This kind of stone facilitated construction of such complex vaults, which involve a transition from a square plan to a rounded octagon and, finally, a semicircular cupola. Above the cupola and under the vaults of the transept, corridors entering the west wall can be reached by spiral staircases housed in the sturdy corner turrets of the transept. These can be used to reach the belfry, for which the toothing stones were laid at the same time, although the tower was not built until construction work began on the nave. On completion of the transept, the future nave was already prepared for by walls whose traces can be detected at the end of the side aisles and above the pillars of the crossing. When construction work was resumed, however, the project had been modified. Building began with the lower parts of the last bay. After that, the nave took on its definitive form and the proportions of the floor plan were made regular. In the four other bays, cruciform pillars with projections support Gothic arches with double rolls, and meet the arch bands from the pointed barrel vault of the chief nave, as well as the round gabled arches between the side aisles, which have segmented half-barrel vaults. For the gutter walls and the facade dressed stone was now replaced by more economical masonry. The more handsome course of medium stone was used only for the structure: pillars, southern windows, northern door, corners and arcades. The walls themselves were made from rag-stone. In the more conspicuous upper parts everything is in dressed stone. This prestigious material was meticulously cut and there are jobber's marks on almost every piece. It adds to the monumentality of the building and enhances its decoration, which is redolent of ancient architecture. On the window level, the pillars are flanked by small Corinthian columns beneath a cornice of acanthus leaves which emphasises the beginning of the vault. As in the transept, the decoration and graceful volumes of the nave reveal the influence of the Burgundian architecture of Cluny. The church was no doubt complete by 1152, when the body of St Trophimus was solemnly translated here. It had been kept at the Alyscamps during reconstruction. An inscription in the side aisle recalls the legend stating that this holy bishop, the church's titular saint (along with St Stephen), was the "apostle of the Gauls". A large crypt was built here for his relics years before but it was destroyed during the reconstruction of the chevet in the Middle Ages.

Relief on the portal.

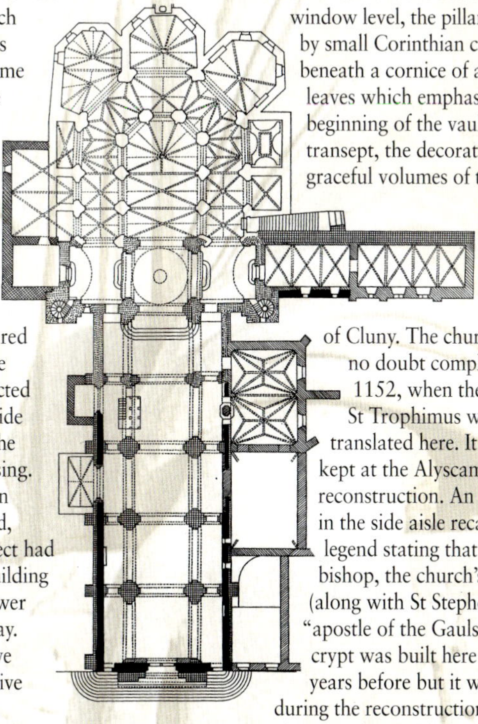

Plan of Saint-Trophime.

Excavations carried out in 1870 showed that the crypt ran under the chevet, the transept and the two last bays of the nave. A.H.-V.

Furniture

DURING THE REVOLUTION, the church was transformed into a Temple of Reason and most of its original furniture was destroyed. However, we can still see the Aubusson tapestries illustrating *The Life of the Virgin*, the painting of *The Stoning of Stephen* by Finsonius, formerly on the high altar (now on the chancel arch) and the altarpiece of the Chapelle des Rois, also by Finsonius.
In the nineteenth century the church was restored by Henri Révoil and Auguste Véran and redecorated with works saved from other churches in Arles that had been demolished during the Revolution. Thus the marble relief representing the *Assumption of the Virgin* (Chapelle Saint-Genest) comes from the Grands Carmes, the marble statue of the Virgin (Chapelle de la Vierge) is from Saint-Honorat des Alyscamps (it was commissioned from the Genoese sculptor Leonardo Mirano in 1618 and venerated under the name of *Notre-Dame de Grâces*) and the *Entombment* (Chapelle du Saint-Sépulcre) is from the church of the Frères-Prêcheurs (Dominicans.)
THREE EARLY CHRISTIAN sarcophagi were also brought into the church during the nineteenth century: one (fourth century), set into the northern gutter-bearing wall, serves as an altar for baptisms: another, the *Sarcophagus of the Crossing of the Red Sea* (fourth century), is in the Chapelle Saint-Genest (northern end of transept), and the third, in the Gothic choir, is the sarcophagus of Geminius (early fifth century), treasurer of the five provinces of Gaul. It was probably made in Ravenna.

The interior of Saint-Trophime.

Detail of portal fresco.

THE RESTORATION work done on Saint-Trophime in the nineteenth century stripped the church of its modern additions and recreated a more medieval style. For example, the polychrome marble pulpit sculpted by Cavalho (1783, Chapelle des Rois) was taken down and replaced by a pulpit designed by Révoil and sculpted by Cantini, with a back and sounding board by Dumas, a cabinetmaker from Arles based in Marseille. It was inaugurated on 16 October 1897. Similarly, the eighteenth-century coffered door was transported to Orange and replaced by the present door with its imitation medieval ironwork. Other elements dating to the nineteenth century are the stained glass windows showing the Holy Virgin, St Trophimus and St Virgilius, all by Maréchal (1875). M.B.

Architecture and external decoration

THE CATHEDRAL is only clearly visible from the west or south. The bell-tower, overlooking the old episcopal quarter, dates from the same period as the nave. Its three levels surmounted by an attic are decorated with Corinthian pilasters and pilaster strips inherited from the eleventh-century Romanesque style. The austere and powerful form of the transept and its corner turrets contrasts with the nave punctuated by buttresses and crowned with a frieze of brackets decorated with foliage, above the chapels added to the side aisles in the late Middle Ages. On the facade, the volumes of the main nave and aisles can still be clearly made out under their sculpted cornices, which form an antique-style pediment at the centre. One can see the difference between the masonry of the lower part and the upper, where the central window is ornamented by a small Corinthian column like those inside.

THE ORIGINALLY plain facade was endowed with one of the most famous portals in southern France in circa 1180. In an excellent state of repair, it is inspired by the main facade of Saint-Gilles-du-Gard and is based on the model of the triumphal arch while also using colonnades of the kind that, in those days, must still have adorned the front of the stage of the nearby Roman theatre. Its rich sculptural decoration makes liberal use of stone taken from ancient monuments. Around the pedestal and central passage a note of colour is provided by luxurious materials such as Carrara marble, black limestone, griotte marble and granite. However, the limestone used for most of the sculpture is itself of excellent quality and may also come from a Roman building.

THE AWARENESS of antiquity manifest above all in the art of the paleochristian sarcophagi is also evident in the style of the figures and plant motifs used here. They were made in a sculptors' workshop and assembled on-site by a team of masons. Old Testament themes are found alongside lions and evil monsters. They are dominated by the statues of the apostles, together with the cathedral's two titular saints, the bishop Trophimus and the deacon Stephen, forced to his knees by the hail of stones from his murderers. On the sides, the *Weighing of Souls* and the hellish monster *Leviathan* warn of the fate of the damned who wait in their chains above a frieze dedicated to the history of the Nativity. As they are led into hell by the devils, the orderly procession of the Elect moves towards Abraham, Isaac and Jacob, next to the twelve apostles on the lintel.

ON THE TYMPANUM, the *Christ in Majesty* surround by the emblems of the Evangelists raises his right hand to them in blessing. The angels surrounding him on the inner side of the archivolt represent the *Adoration of the Lamb of the Apocalypse* at the end of time, as announced by the angels with their keyed trumpets. A.H.-V.

Portal of Saint-Trophime. Drawing by Yacine Azzoug.

Saint-Trophime Cloister

Place de la République

Access via the Palais de l'Archevêché

Open:

2 Nov. - 28 Feb.: 10.00 -17.00

1 March - 30 April : 9.00-18.00

2 May - 30 Sept.: 9.00-19.00

1 Oct. - 31 Oct.: 9.00-18.00

Facing: inside the cloister. Below: the cloister and, behind it, the Tour Gioffredi.

In the twelfth and thirteenth centuries, the area south of the cathedral was filled by two large ensembles: in line with the facade of the nave, the archbishop's palace (replaced by a Baroque construction in the seventeenth century), and to the south, a Gothic wing following the line of the Roman wall.

Building the cloister

CONSTRUCTION of this Romanesque ensemble, which may have taken the place of older buildings, began with a first edifice abutting the southern arm of the transept and built in the manner of the lower parts of the nave. It was extended southwards by a large timbered refectory with a vaulted cellar, and eastwards by the first chapter house. Plans for a cloister surrounded by vaulted walks, or galleries, were not made until the mid-twelfth century. Running alongside another barrel-vaulted hall, the chapter house was, at the end of the twelfth century, decorated with a rich facade on the side of the northern walk, which was the first of two Romanesque walks built here. The eastern walk, conceived along with the dormitory wing, dates from the early thirteenth century. The project was never completed and so the planned superstructure was never added to the buttress-cum-pilasters of the pillars that punctuate the arcades. The last two walks with their ribbed vaults and the large Gothic portal in the cloister's southern wall were not built until 1370-1380.

Decoration of the walks

THE DECORATION of the Romanesque walks, which is very close to that of the portal from the same period, is exceptionally rich.

Set on geminate columns, the arcades are in groups of four, placed between pillars that support the transverse ribs of the barrel vaults. The vault is described as rampant because the sumptuous figured consoles in the perimeter walls that support it on each side are at different heights. The variety of geminate columns reflects the desire to mix round and polygonal forms, which were often cut from the same single block of stone. Fine Corinthian capitals combined with figured motifs alternate with historiated capitals, most of them illustrating the Old Testament (north side) and the Life of Christ (east side).
NORTHERN WALK. – In the northern walk *Abraham's Hospitality and Sacrifice,* the *Giving of the Old and New Law,* the *Prophet Balaam* and the *Raising of Lazarus identify* God's Chosen People and announce the promise of eternal life. The reliefs on the four northern pillars relate the Resurrection of Christ. Four marble figures cut from reused blocks of unequal size represent *Christ Appearing to the Pilgrims of Emmaus* and *Doubting Thomas* on the intermediary pillars, and the two titular saints, Trophimus and Stephen, forming the "cornerstones" of the building. As on the portal, Trophimus and Stephen are accompanied by the Apostles John, Peter, Paul and Andrew.
EASTERN WALK. – In the eastern walk, where Gothic influences are already in evidence, the same arrangement is used for the *Christ of the Flagellation* and for the *Cross,* the remains of which can still be made out on the second intermediary pillar between the figures of the *Church* and *St John the Evangelist in Mourning,* often identified as Solomon and the Queen of Sheba. The capitals reprise some of the Nativity cycle on the portal, with striking formal analogies that are also evident in the previous gallery, in spite of stylistic differences. In the spandrels of the profiled arcades the *Wise Virgins Announce the Return of the Groom.* In the southern corner pillar, the iconographic cycle is brought to a close by the *Baptism of Christ,* the *Temptation in the Wilderness* and the *Last Supper.*

The Gothic galleries

The last two walks (southern and western), which are rib-vaulted, and the large Gothic portal in the southern cloister wall, were not built until around 1370-1380.
SOUTHERN WALK. – The the older of the two walks, its pillars have recesses which formerly held statuettes. The sculptures on the capitals illustrate the life of St Trophimus, as related in a poem written in around 1225.
WESTERN WALK. – The iconography here is less coherent than in the other galleries. Biblical episodes mix with popular local themes in which new devotions feature prominently, with the

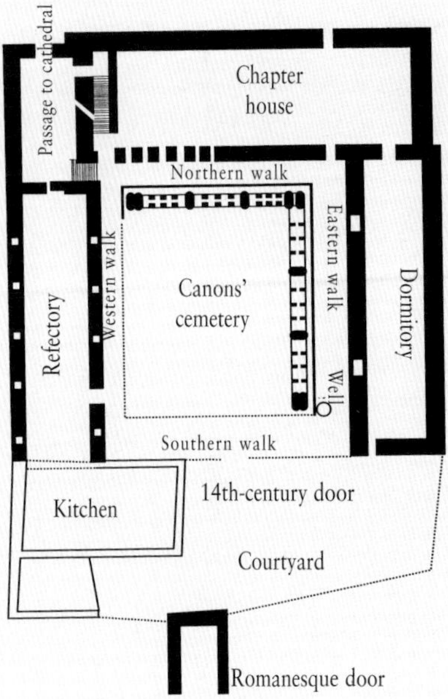

Coronation of the Virgin and the cult of the Saints of Bethany. A.H.-V.

The tapestries of the chapter house

The first series represents a scene from the *Life of the Virgin* and belongs to a set hung in Saint-Trophime. These seventeenth-century Aubusson tapestries are decorated in the Flemish style.
THE OTHER series, of unknown provenance, dates from the early eighteenth century. Its theme is *Jerusalem Delivered* and, particularly, the Life of Godfrey of Bouillon, king of Jerusalem in the eleventh century. M.B.-C.B.

1. Medieval gate, cloister.
2. Archbishop's palace.

Gate of the Provost's house

Rue du Cloître

THE CLOSED SPACE of the canons' *claustrum* was entered at the southern end through a superb portal (late twelfth century) which was subsequently incorporated into the facade of the Provost's house (Maison du Prévôt). With decoration similar to that of a church portal, the gate is a monumental version of the door to the old refectory (cloister, west walk). On either side, a Corinthian column on a pedestal replaces the corners of the jambshafts. Their profiled and sculpted abutments are surmounted by bare blocks. Supporting the simple tympanum, a finely bonded flat arch lintel spans the wide passageway. A fine archivolt with two rows of arch-stones recalls the prestigious model of Roman city gates. A prestigious construction referring to the city's ancient past, this gateway to the canons' quarter was thus much more than a simple point of access: it recalled the former grandeur and rank of the metropolitan Church and its chapter. A.H.-V.

Palais de l'Archevêché

Place de la République

IN THE MIDDLE AGES an archbishop's palace was built in line with the facade of Saint-Trophime, although all visible trace of it has now disappeared. In the twelfth century, it was extended by the Tour Gioffredi. Built on the site now occupied by the post office building, this tower was a key part of the buildings enclosing the canons' quarter at the southwest end. Abutting this corner stood the Porte Sainte-Étienne, the gateway to the city, which was demolished in 1810.

THE PALACE underwent numerous transformations. One of the main ones was carried out by Monseigneur de Grignan, who totally recast it in the second half of the seventeenth century. This was when the building acquired its entrance porch, monumental stairway and room structure whose decoration, with the fireplace and wall paintings, constitutes a fine example of the classical style in Arles.

IN 1786, Monseigneur de Lau decided to rebuild the facade in the plain Classical style that we can still see here today.

From the archbishop's palace to the university offices

THE REVOLUTIONARY PERIOD radically changed the function of this palace which was home to the archbishop when residing in Arles as well to such distinguished visitors as Madame de Sévigné and her daughter Madame de Grignan. In 1790 the archbishopric and the cathedral chapter were abolished by the Constituent Assembly. And when the Concordat of 1801 failed to reinstate them, the archbishopric was definitively absorbed into that of Aix-en-Provence. From 1793 to 1794 the palace housed the district administration. Under the First Empire it was shared by the parish clergy and the gendarmerie. They were succeeded by the municipal library in 1829. When this in turn moved to the Espace Van Gogh, the former archbishop's buildings became the home of the university administration. M.B.

Central Arles
The conservation area

IN HIS SPEECH introducing a new law on listed areas, passed on 4 August 1962, French Minister of Culture André Malraux warned that "If we allow these old banks of the Seine redolent of Romantic lithographs to be destroyed, it will be like banishing from Paris the spirit of Daumier and the shade of Baudelaire." The same can be said of the banks of the Rhône at Arles, which were so famously illustrated by the paintings of Vincent Van Gogh.

IF THE CONCEPT of the historic monument goes back a long way, the notion of urban heritage dates only from the late nineteenth century and did not really come into its own until the mid-twentieth.

Facade of the Hôtel Courtois de Langlade.

A conservation area since 1966, the historic centre of Arles is fully worthy of such consideration. The city's urban heritage is often hidden, buried. Here and there we can trace the town's development on the unchanging grid of the *cardo* (Rue de l'Hôtel de Ville) and *decumanus* (Rue de la Calade). Then there is the barely perceptible interlocking of the Roman forum and today's housing blocks (vestiges of the temple on today's Place du Forum). The architectural riches of Arles are epitomised by the Rue Peytret, which has buildings dating from the fourteenth to the nineteenth century.

WHATEVER their inherent importance, these historic buildings are also part of a large-scale urban composition testifying to the necessary articulation of monumental and urban heritages. This is most striking on the Place de la République, where we are affected by the spatial harmony as much as by the monuments themselves.

VISITORS will get a better idea of this quality as they walk around the squares of the city centre, whose charm is entirely due to their composition and to the fact that one comes across them unexpectedly –when turning a corner. Places Balechou, Louis-Blanc and Patras all deserve a mention here, as does the Place the de la Redoute.

GETTING to know and understand Arles also means having a good sense of its various components, such as the successive walls that bore witness to the ups and downs of its history. In the La Major quarter, the Rue Renan follows the ground plan of the Roman ramparts in the middle of the plot. They were demolished in order to allow construction of the amphitheatre. The Rue Tour-de-Fabre corresponds to the plan of another, later wall. Walking down the Rue du Cloître we can tell that we are leaving the area of the episcopal city because of the gate. Similarly, in the Rue du Grand-Couvent, we realise that we are following the wall of the Saint-Césaire house.

WHEN ARGUING the case for his law on conservation areas, Malraux hoped that it would make it possible to balance conservation and preservation with modernity, the construction of the cities of tomorrow. This is why the law made provision for financial incentives and tax breaks.

ARLES HAS ALWAYS understood the spirit of Malraux's reform. The town's planning policy has included programmes for the rehabilitation of housing for all sectors of the population while ensuring that the town centre remains well provided with shops and services. B.S.

1. Église Sainte-Anne.
2. Old post office building.
3. The obelisk and fountain.

Opposite the Église Saint-Trophime stands the Église Sainte-Anne.

Église Sainte-Anne *or* Notre-Dame-la-Principale

Place de la République

UNDER THE Ancien Régime, Notre-Dame-la-Principale was the parish church of the town centre. First rebuilt as early as 1175, the church was again on the brink of collapse by the early seventeenth century. In 1613 the archbishop of Arles, Monseigneur du Laurens, ordered reconstruction. The new edifice, with its marked throwback to the old southern Gothic style, was set back from the square so that the area could be renovated. Work finished in 1627, and the church was consecrated on St Anne's Day. Indeed, it was dedicated to St Anne and housed her relics, stored in a vermeil bust. Ministry was performed by priests of the Oratorian congregation, who were present in Arles from 1617 onwards. THE INTERIOR, handled in the Gothic style, has a nave with five bays and side chapels. At the west end, the choir has a pentagonal apse. None of the original furniture remains here. On the facade can be seen traces of two armorial bearings hammered onto it during the Revolution: the arms of France and those of the city. Above the door, in a recess, was a statue of the Virgin, which was replaced by bust of Minerva when the Musée Lapidaire was located here. The building was in fact deconsecrated after the Revolution and replaced as parish church by Saint-Trophime, which at the same time lost its cathedral status. By an imperial decree of 1805, the church of Sainte-Anne was donated to the town to be made into a museum and store for works of art. This was done in 1825-1826 and the old church became the Musée Lapidaire d'Art Païen until its collections were transferred to the Musée de l'Arles Antique in 1994. Today, the former church of Sainte-Anne is a cultural centre for temporary exhibitions. M.B.

Ancien Hôtel des Postes

Place de la République

TO THE RIGHT of the archbishop's palace, the building formerly occupied by the post office was built in 1898 by the local architects Auguste Véran and his son Léon. Bearing witness to the importance of the public services at the time, the Hôtel des Postes is built in the eclectic style characteristic of the late nineteenth century. A number of the decorative elements on the facade echo those of the seventeenth-century town hall building, notably the pediment and the balusters around the roof. O.C.

The Obelisk

Place de la République

ROMAN CIRCUSES, which were used mainly for chariot races and hunting, contained a large track divided in two by a structure called a *spina*, or "spine", consisting of two separate and parallel walls reinforced in places by struts. The *spina* was abundantly decorated with statues and pools and fitted with equipment such as posts at the ends (the

2

3

charioteers tried to pass as close as they could without breaking the axles of their chariots), a structure made of seven bronze dolphins which was used to mark the number of laps and, finally, an obelisk, a solar and imperial symbol which also guided the charioteers. This obelisk was erected in Arles during the reign of the Emperor Constantine in the centre of what was then the *spina*. For many years a mystery, analysis of its stone recently traced its origins to a Roman quarry in Turkey. After the circus was abandoned in the sixth century, the obelisk crumbled and broke in two. It was rediscovered in 1389 and, in the centuries to come, important visitors would regularly be taken to see it. Henri IV entertained the idea of putting it in the middle of the amphitheatre. His plans were partially adopted by the town's aldermen in 1675, when they decided to raise the obelisk on the royal square, "to the greater glory of King Louis XIV". It took forty days to transport the piece, with huge resources deployed for a journey of only a few hundred metres. But the hardest part was still to come: placing the shaft on the pedestal designed by the architect Jacques Peytret. The city enlisted the help of sailors specialised in handling ship's masts. On 26 March 1676, the operation was completed with installation of the tip. Now the royal symbol, a blue-bronze globe scattered with fleurs-de-lys surmounted by a golden sun, could be placed on the tip. Other emblems would follow, reflecting the political regime at the time: the Phrygian cap of the revolutionaries, Napoleon's eagle, the cockerel of the Orléanist monarchy, the eagle of the Second Empire and, again, the royal sun. This last item was removed in 1866 and now adorns the courtyard of the Musée Réattu. C.S.

Hôtel de Ville

Place de la République

In 1657, the city council decided to build a new town hall on the site of the old one, which stood between the Maison du Roi (King's House, formerly the Palais des Podestats) and the clock tower, which the consuls intended to preserve, and which still rises above the town hall today. This tower was built between 1543 and 1558 in place of an older tower. It was fitted with four clocks, of which only one has survived. The architectural structure of the clock tower and its antique-style decoration both imitate the Roman mausoleum at Saint-Rémy-de-Provence, but its architecture is still characteristic of the refined Provençal Renaissance style.
A number of different projects were put forward by local architects in response to the aldermen's decision, but none of them made it beyond the drawing board. In 1666 work began on a design by La Valfenière, who was based in Avignon, but it was abandoned several months later and the walls, now several metres high, were razed. It was only in 1673 that work started on the building we know today. The definitive plan resulted from

1

collaboration between Jacques Peytret, an architect from Arles and the Parisian Jules Hardouin-Mansart.

MANSART, then architect to the King, had in fact been passing through Arles in June 1673 when he was asked to give his opinion of Peytret's project and to suggest the best way of vaulting the large hall planned for the ground floor. He suggested a different way of building the stairwell and did not hesitate to completely hide the clocktower between the north and east facades. Apart from these modifications, he made few major changes to the plans drawn up by his colleague in Arles and kept the idea of a vaulted hall. The vault can still be admired today as a masterpiece of Classical stone-cutting. It is formed by two perpendicular barrel vaults of differing widths with three-centred lunettes.

At the sides of the hall the vault is supported by double columns. The main staircase leading to the council chamber is framed by two stone lions.

THE SOLUTION recommended by Hardouin-Mansart to ensure that the vault built over the hall would be safe, which was to divide the hall into two unequal parts, met with a far from enthusiastic response from the Consuls. In fact, they called on several local architects and masons for further advice. But, since the opinions expressed to them were all favourable, the city council ruled in September 1674 that work could begin on the vault over the hall in accordance with plans drawn up by Peytret and under the direction of Hardouin-Mansart. At this point, construction of the edifice had already reached the cornice on the second floor. Agreement had been reached on the price (prix-fait) of the framework, which was also designed by Peytret. Work on the building continued without interruption through to March 1676, when it was completed.

THE GENERAL approach here is consistent with the French tradition of prestige architecture. The town hall has three storeys. The first of these is treated

2

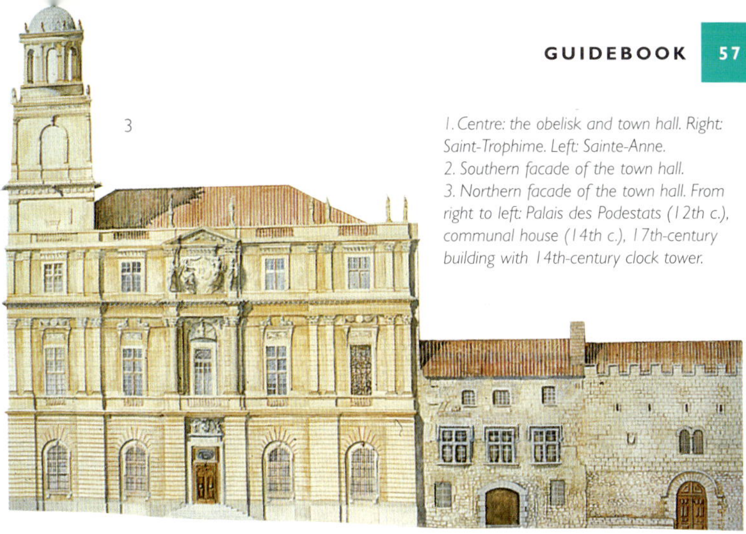

1. Centre: the obelisk and town hall. Right: Saint-Trophime. Left: Sainte-Anne.
2. Southern facade of the town hall.
3. Northern facade of the town hall. From right to left: Palais des Podestats (12th c.), communal house (14th c.), 17th-century building with 14th-century clock tower.

like a base with bossage decoration. The second floor, or piano nobile, has an imposing decorative scheme at the centre with double columns framing a French window giving onto a balcony with a stone balustrade. The third floor is dominated by a central pediment featuring a sun, the symbol of Louis XIV, and a decorative scheme of balusters and fireballs. The bulk of the sculpted stone decoration, both internal and external, was entrusted to Jean Dedieu. In 1674 he made the two lions on the main staircase, the masks on the windows, the coats of arms on the vestibule door, the king's and the city's ciphers and the six medallions of the Kings of Arles (which were destroyed during the Revolution) for the windows on the first floor. The following year Dedieu sculpted the decoration of the two facades, the two large royal coats of arms, the decorated pediments, the trophies of arms and the fifteen vases of the terminal balustrade. Of the four large statues that he undertook to make, only the figures of Strength and Justice on the northern facade can still be seen today. The two sitting captives that were originally on the trophies of the southern facade have been lost. They were no doubt removed during the Revolution.
INSIDE, the council chamber has kept its fine wooden decoration, made in the eighteenth century by Laurent Bondon, a sculptor from Avignon who also executed the ceiling. This ceiling is adorned with medallions representing the ancient monuments of Arles painted by Mandon de Cazan. The ornaments in relief were painted and gilded by Antoine Reynaud, another artist from Avignon. Above the panelling fluted Corinthian pilasters flank trophies of arms and musical instruments. The frames adorning the chamber are integrated into the woodwork. These now house paintings done by Jean Roche in around 1920. O.C. [AFTER JEAN BOYER]

We now come to the Plan de la Cour. Located to the northern side of the town hall, which is where the main entrance used to be (the southern side of the square was then very small), this *plan*, or square, was laid with fine polychrome paving in the eighteenth century. Standing on the facing pavement, you can observe the developments in municipal architecture: on the right, the Palais des Podestats from the thirteenth century, then the municipal building erected in the fifteenth with its fine mullion and transom windows, and finally the large seventeenth-century classical building.

Palais des Podestats

Plan de la Cour

IN THE EARLY thirteenth century, Arles was under the domination of the archbishop, the count, its lords and the Consuls. From 1220 to 1235 the community was governed by a foreigner, the *podestat*, often an Italian, appointed for a year.
THE PALAIS des Podestats dates from the thirteenth century. At the end of the Middle Ages it was the residence of the *viguier* (a kind of judge, or provost) and housed the *comtal* (count's) court. The facade has a fortified look with its

1

2

1. Palais des Podestats.
2. Hôtel de Viguier.
3. Hôtel de Vernon.
4. Hôtel des Amazones (detail).
5. Hôtel Forbin-Soliers.

crenellations and loopholes, featuring twin windows with round arches and a Romanesque porch. To the left can be seen the "bench of justice" where the comtal officers sat when they took the oath to respect the city's privileges, and where declarations and sentences were read out. In the courtyard, where the buildings were much altered as a result of the reorganisation of the municipal offices, we can still see, on the left, the old dungeons and some interesting graffiti on the wall facing the porch. O.C. [AFTER LOUIS STOUFF]

Retracing our steps, we come to the beginning of the Rue de l'Hôtel-de-Ville.

Hôtel de Viguier

31, Rue de l'Hôtel-de-Ville

THE HÔTEL de Viguier originally belonged to one of Arles' oldest noble families, the La Tours, and the interior (from the late sixteenth century) still shows traces of the work they had done here. The buildings was later purchased by another noble family, the Viguiers, no doubt in the seventeenth century. In 1761 the facade of the townhouse was rebuilt as part of a works programme to realign the street. Typically of late eighteenth-century facades in Arles, the building's only external decorative elements are the cornice and the brackets that set off the door. O.C.

Towards the middle of the Rue de l'Hôtel-de-Ville, on the right, we come to the Rue des Arènes. This follows the slope of the hill. In Roman times the road led to the forum and amphitheatre. In the sixteenth century the construction of large numbers of townhouses established the street as one of Arles' most aristocratic areas. On the left we see the Rue Vernon and the former Hôtel de Vernon.

Hôtel de Vernon

5, Rue Vernon

IN 1711, Guillaume de Vernon married Anne du Port whose dowry was this townhouse, known since the sixteenth century. It became the main post office building in the nineteenth century. It then belonged to the Remacle family (Louis Remacle was mayor of Arles from 1871 to 1872) and after them to the Dervieux. It has a broad classical facade on three levels typical of early eighteenth-century townhouses in Arles. In addition to the quality of the construction and overall harmony, we should note the fine decoration of the door frame and its bracketed cornice, and also the quality of the woodwork. Inside, the building has conserved the staircase, layout and ceilings from the seventeenth and eighteenth centuries. O.C.

We now come back to the Rue des Arènes. With the refined rhythm of its curving forms, the decoration of the first townhouse on the right (33, Rue des Arènes) is inspired by the Italian Renaissance. Next-door stands the Hôtel Forbin-Soliers.

Hôtel Forbin-Soliers

31, Rue des Arènes

THE HÔTEL Forbin-Soliers belonged to the illustrious Forbin family, whose

3

4

5

various members were prominent figures in the cities of Avignon and Aix as well as Arles. The building was extensively restored in the nineteenth century by the architect Auguste Véran. The upper level of this three-storey mansion has some fine sixteenth-century Renaissance decorative elements done in the antique style, including fluted pilasters and Corinthian capitals. The échauguette, or watchtower, has kept its original features, with small windows framed by Corinthian pilasters resting on sculpted consoles. Usually fitted with a small spiral staircase leading to a terrace, such watchtowers were a common feature of the city's fifteenth- and sixteenth-century buildings. O.C.

Hôtel des Amazones

29, Rue des Arènes

THE HÔTEL des Amazones was built in the sixteenth century for the canon Melchior de Sanson-Malcane. Its three storeys are surmounted by an attic. Elements of the building's Renaissance decoration can still be seen on the Rue Balechou side, where a moulded cornice resting on sculpted brackets delimits the first and second floors, and the upper level has a frieze with metopes and triglyphs.

ONE OF the two low reliefs ornamenting this facade shows Amazons fighting. Such details reveal how interested the people of Arles were in their Roman past. The facade on the Rue des Arènes side was completely rebuilt in the eighteenth century. O.C.

Hôtel de Castillon

20, Rue des Arènes

FACING the Hôtel des Amazones stands one of the biggest private mansions in Arles. The building became the property of Charles de Castillon in the fifteenth century. It has a fine three-storeyed facade in the classical style, which was manifestly reworked in later centuries. Although several of them have been walled up, the first-floor windows are particularly fine with their large voussoirs. The last floor is rendered as an attic, with regular, almost square openings framed by pilasters. Traces of earlier buildings are still visible in the small central courtyard, which is entered via the street porch. Although it has now been converted into flats, the interior still has a few of the old French-style ceilings. O.C.

Hôtel Quiqueran de Beaujeu

École Nationale de la Photographie

16, Rue des Arènes

Tel. 04.90.99.33.33

Fax 04.90.99.33.59

THE QUIQUERAN de Beaujeus were a powerful local family from the old nobility. They acquired this townhouse in the mid-eighteenth century and undertook major renovation work, rebuilding the western facade on today's Rue Doisneau. The decorative work on the main, southern facade is highly refined. It has regularly spaced windows with handsome moulded frames and is surmounted by a large triangular

1. Hôtel Quiqueran de Beaujeu.
2. Hôtel Bouchet de Faucon.

pediment. This facade and the two wings shelter a large courtyard which is reached from the street through an imposing porch similar to those found on Parisian townhouses. In addition to the felicitously preserved external decoration, the interior of the mansion also boasts a fine staircase with a wrought iron handrail. Now home to the École Nationale de la Photographie, the Hôtel Quiqueran de Beaujeu has all the charm and majesty of the finest eighteenth-century townhouses.

École Nationale de la Photographie (ENP)

THIS NATIONAL photography school is supervised by the French Ministry of Culture. To be eligible for admission, students must have two years' experience of higher education. Applicants are selected by exam. The school boasts a distinguished teaching staff and also runs an artist-in-residence scheme. Students here have the possibility of undertaking international exchanges and study trips. Exhibitions are put on in the School's own gallery. The three-year curriculum leads to a higher diploma in photography.

Just after the Hôtel Quiqueran de Beaujeu we turn into the Rue Aristide-Briand. Towards the end of this street, on the left, stands another large townhouse, which is now municipal property.

Hôtel Bouchet de Faucon

3, Rue Aristide-Briand

LOUIS DE BOUCHET DE FAUCON, a councillor at the Parliament of Provence, bought this townhouse in 1769 when his family's power was at its apogee. Dating back to the sixteenth century, the three-storey building has been extensively renovated. The facade, built in typical Classical style, sports a portal with Ionic pilasters as well as a good number of curved windows and a large moulded pediment whose monogram, RF, reminds us that the building, now occupied by municipal services, once housed the sub-prefecture. On the first floor a French window opening onto a wrought iron balcony is surmounted by a chock representing a woman's head accompanied by a garland of flowers. The central section and the extremities of the walls are highlighted by prominent stone piers and quoins. O.C.

Standing almost directly opposite the Hôtel Bouchet de Faucon we see a house surmounted by a curious sculpture possibly representing two interlacing salamanders. This was the home of the younger son of the wealthy Barras family, whose main residence was located not far from the Église des Dominicains. Going back up the Rue Aristide-Briand, and then left into the Rue Faure, we come to the Rue Raspail where a porch with a basket-handle arch is a reminder of the old Ursuline convent.

Couvent des Ursulines

14, Rue Raspail

IN 1617, Jeanne Rampalle founded a congregation of Ursuline nuns in Arles and in the same year a convent was established near the amphitheatre.

1

2

1. Couvent des Ursulines.
2. Sculpture on the facade of the Grande Boucherie.

Among the young women who entered this order based on the rule of St Augustine we find the names of such prominent local families as the Cadenets, the Nicolays and the Mandons. In 1789 the community consisted of only four or five nuns. They were expelled in 1792 and the church and convent were sold off, along with their furniture and ornaments. The church consisted of a simple nave with one lateral chapel on the south side dedicated to the Holy Cross. Most of the buildings were destroyed but vestiges can still be seen from the Impasse des Ursulines, notably some fifteenth- and sixteenth-century windows from an earlier building. M.B.

Retracing our steps now and heading down the Rue Raspail, we come to the Rue du 4-Septembre. This street is an important thoroughfare between the Cavalerie quarter and the Cité. To its west lies the Grande Boucherie.

Grande Boucherie
Salle Jean-et-Pons-Dedieu

62, Rue du 4-Septembre

THE GRANDE BOUCHERIE was where local shopkeepers bought their wholesale supplies of meat. Records of the site go back to the Middle Ages.

IN 1724, the consuls commissioned the architect and sculptor Antoine II Guibert to build a new market hall. The frontage, which is characteristic of French functional architecture in the first half of the eighteenth century, has three big openings onto the street with semicircular arches. The building's function is spelt out very clearly by the decorative ox and ram heads, horns of plenty and butcher's tools sculpted by Pons Dedieu.

FROM the interwar years until around 1970 the Grande Boucherie housed a well-known local cinema, *Le Studio*. It is now used as a meeting and conference hall. O.C.

Taking a short detour through the alley on the other side of the street to the right, then turning left down the Rue des Suisses, we get a view of one of Arles' most curious facades, in the Rue Peytret.

Rue Peytret

IN THIS street we can find a real historical anthology of architectural styles in Arles, with several dozen metres of facades featuring thirteenth century geminate and trefoil windows, mullion windows, windows renovated during the eighteenth century and the traces of entrances to craftsmen's shops or workshops. The house on the right of the street has kept part of its old medieval facade. It is very tall and divided into three levels: on the left, the ground floor still has a few keystones from an old door with a semicircular arch. On the first floor we can see the remains of two series of geminate windows with trefoil arches set within Gothic arches and resting on a sawteeth frieze. The final floor, below the attic, is pierced with five series of geminate windows with trefoil arches. The ensemble was built in fine dressed stone which is still in good condition on the right-hand side of the facade. The interior was totally transformed as a result of the construction of the new facade on the Rue des Suisses during the seventeenth century. V.E.

1

1. Église Saint-Julien.
2. Hôtel de Grille.

We now retrace our steps. Further down, on the corner of the Rue du 4-Septembre and the Rue de Grille, stands the Hôtel de Grille.

Hôtel de Grille

14, Rue de Grille

THE HÔTEL de Grille is eminently representative of the Louis XIV style in urban architecture. The facade overlooking the Rue de Grille is typical of prestige buildings of the classical period. It has a central section decorated with double columns, bracketed cornices and a pediment. This part of the townhouse was built in 1691 by François de Grille d'Estoublon, the descendent of a rich Italian family that settled in Arles in the fifteenth century and climbed swiftly up the social ladder. The interior still features the late seventeenth-century staircase. The roof is edged with a balustrade and fireballs. O.C.

2

Going eastwards down the Rue du 4-Septembre, we now head towards the Église Saint-Julien.

Église Saint-Julien

Rue du 4-Septembre

THE FIRST church dedicated to St Julian is thought to have been consecrated by Pope Calixtus II (1119-1124) on his way back from the Council of Reims. Little is known about this church except that, in addition to St Julian the Hospitaller, it is linked with St Anthony, whose relics were deposited there on 8 January 1490. Reconstruction was decided in 1647 because the church was judged too small and ramshackle. In January 1662 Monseigneur de Grignan consecrated the new building which, as late as the mid-seventeenth century, maintained the southern Gothic style.

RANSACKED during the Revolution, then re-established by the Concordat in 1801, Saint-Julien apparently survived with no further upheavals until the bombing of 1944, which left it severely damaged. The town council considered demolition, but thanks to the dogged determination of the curate Saint-Julien was rebuilt. Today it is no longer a parish church, but it continues to play a role and houses the annual mass for the santonniers, makers of traditional Provençal figures.

IN 1944 nearly all the furniture was destroyed, along with the historiated stained glass by Guilbert d'Annelle, the most important work of this kind done in Arles in the nineteenth century. All that remains of the eighteenth-century furniture is the fine gilded altarpiece in the choir, donated by the Brotherhood of the Holy Sacrament. In addition to the painting of *St Julian the Hospitaller* by Parrocel (1686), note the marble Virgin attributed to Révoil, a student of David, and a *Way of the Cross* painted in 1958 by Guy Renne. M.B.

We now take the Rue de l'Amphithéâtre on our right, noting its seventeenth and eighteenth-century bourgeois houses on our way to the amphitheatre.

Amphitheatre

Rond-Point des Arènes	
Open:	
2 Nov. - 28 Feb.: 10.00 - 17.00	
1 March - 30 April: 9.00-18.00	
2 May - 30 Sept.: 9.00-19.00	
1 Oct. - 31 Oct.: 9.00-18.00	

The amphitheatre was built at the northern end of the Roman town on the northern slopes of the Hauture hill. It dominates the quarter that stretches down to the Rhône, which was known in medieval times as the Bourg-Neuf. Its orientation, which is out of line with the general plan of the ancient city, is no doubt due to a slight depression in the hill. This topographical constraint means that the underlying rock is at surface level at the western end of the amphitheatre while being several metres below ground at the northeastern end. This has allowed for the preservation of a number of earlier vestiges.

16th-century print of the amphitheatre.

View over the town and the Rhône from the amphitheatre.

In order to build the amphitheatre it was necessary first of all to take down part of the old city wall, which probably dated back to the Augustan period. The presence of these remains provide our first clue when it comes to dating the amphitheatre itself. A stylistic study reveals similarities with the Coliseum, which was built some years earlier. This amphitheatre was

thus most probably built in the last decade of the first century AD, a period when, as is attested by archaeological evidence elsewhere in the city, Arles grew considerably.

AT THE END of antiquity townspeople began building houses for themselves inside the structure and it was soon being used as a safe refuge for the population. Its fortifications were strengthened during the Middle Ages by four towers, which gave the amphitheatre the unusual appearance we know today. The Roman structure now constituted a small town in its own right, complete with a public square in the centre and a chapel containing the relics of St Genesius, Arles' own martyr, who is honoured as the patron of notaries. Eighteenth-century attempts at redevelopment came to nothing. However, the amphitheatre was totally cleared between 1823 and 1844.

BECAUSE OF this chequered career, the amphitheatre has come down to us in a very incomplete state. Most of the tiers have been lost and the internal gallery on the first floor has survived only on the eastern side. The upper level, which is so well preserved in nearby Nîmes, has been partially salvaged, and extends down to the outward surface of the openings on the first floor.

MEASURING 136 metres from end to end and 107 metres across, this oval arena is slightly larger than the one in Nîmes and comes twentieth in a ranking of amphitheatres in the Roman world. The facade is 21 metres high and has two rows of sixty arcades with round arches separated by massive, orthogonal section jambshafts. Wider openings are used to highlight the lengthways and crossways axes of the oval. Originally the main entrance was not at the northern end, as it is today, but on the western side, where we can see remains of a staircase overlooking the city.

THE *CAVEA* (spectators' area) comprised 34 tiers and was divided up into four sections (*maeniana*), one for each of the different social ranks. Since the seats were all 40 centimetres wide, we can therefore estimate that the amphitheatre had a capacity of 21,000. The upper part of the *cavea* has been destroyed but the tiers originally rose continuously from the podium up to the top of the edifice and the attic, which has also been destroyed. In order to enable spectators to reach the different tiers, the building was designed with an ingenious system in which circular galleries alternated with horizontal passages and stairs.

THE EXTERNAL ground floor gallery is particularly remarkable, notably for its covering of huge monolithic slabs. It gave access to an internal gallery with a semicircular vault that opened onto the first *maenianum* and onto the lower part of the second. Stairways leading from the external gallery afforded access to the first entresol from which one could reach either the second *maenianum* or the external gallery on the first floor. Also fully vaulted, this gallery is lower than the one on the ground floor. From here one could either take the stairs to the third

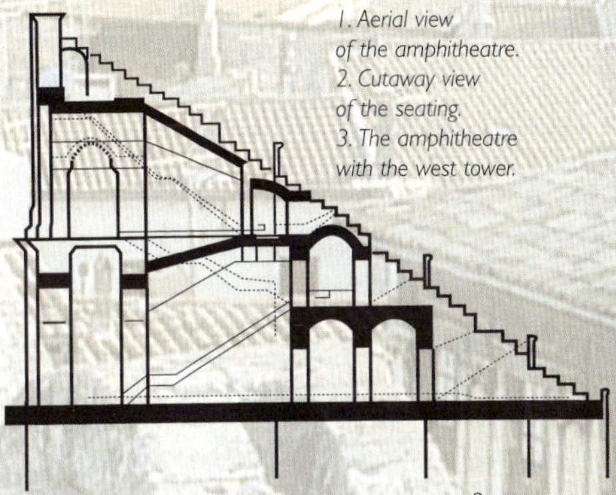

2

3

1. Aerial view of the amphitheatre. 2. Cutaway view of the seating. 3. The amphitheatre with the west tower.

maenianum, or, via a horizontal landing, reach a second entresol from which a stairway led to the attic, which constituted the fourth *maenianum.*

THE CENTRAL area, which was where the games took place, was separated from the tiers by a carefully constructed wall called the podium. It is covered with large slabs of stone on which we can still make out traces of an inscription praising the generosity of some local magistrate. The podium is pierced with four doorways: two smaller ones on the shorter axis of the oval and two larger ones at the northern and southern ends. Their thresholds now stand about two metres above the current level of the ground. The reason for this is that the arena originally had a wooden floor whose lathes were supported by stone reaching to the top of the podium's lower section. The numerous walls and pedestals which ensured the floor's stability also left sufficient room for the various stage machines and scenery required for the games. In fact, the plan of the ground floor with its circular galleries is at least partially duplicated in the basement. These underground spaces communicated with the basement proper, thus forming what is a unique structure when compared to other Roman amphitheatres.

WHEREAS the theatre was used for performances of a "cultural" nature, the amphitheatre was the place for combat, pitting either gladiator against gladiator or gladiators against wild beasts. These fights were put on during feast days and usually financed by local magistrates whose careers could often hinge on such shows of largesse.

THE GLADIATORS came from a variety of backgrounds. Alongside the criminals who had been condemned to death or forced labour there were also volunteers attracted by prospects of gold or glory, but also no doubt by the danger. Combats would continue until the death of one of the adversaries. If a gladiator conceded defeat he would throw himself on the mercy of the public who, by raising or turning down their thumbs would decide on life or death. Thumbs down meant execution, in which case the victor would cut his adversary's throat and be awarded the victor's laurels plus a large sum of money. If, after at least five years of service, a gladiator had managed to stay alive he would be set free. M.H.

1

1. Hôtel Barrême de Manville.
2. Hôtel de Donines.

2

We now take the pedestrian section of the road on the western side of the amphitheatre.

Église Saint-Michel-de-l'Escale

Rond-Point des Arènes

DURING the long years when the amphitheatre was a residential area, it contained two religious buildings. Nothing now remains of the church of Saint-Genest, which stood among the houses. As for the medieval church of Saint-Michel, a small Romanesque window visible from outside the amphitheatre, near the Rue du Grand-Couvent, indicates that some of it must have occupied part of the western tower. The main building stood, though, stood in an arcade. The church was reached by a steep stairway or a ladder. It is mentioned in bequests from 1234 and 1238. It was demolished when the amphitheatre was cleared. O.C.

Hôtel Barrême de Manville

10, Rond-Point des Arènes

THIS TOWNHOUSE was bought in 1743 by Charles de Barrême de Manville, ajurist. The facade is from the second half of the eighteenth century. It is elegantly decorated with straight architraves, large pilasters with Ionic capitals and balconies with balusters. The seventeenth-century interior and courtyard are highly refined. Note the stone balustrades around the terraces. Until recently, this mansion housed a photography festival, the Rencontres Internationales d'Arles. O.C.

Hôtel de Luppé

24 bis, Rond-Point des Arènes

THIS TOWNHOUSE looks rather like a Roman palazzo. The very eye-catching facade was in fact built in the early twentieth century by Gaston de Luppé, a scholar with a real passion for Italy. It has Gothic-Arab windows and above the loggia the roof is supported by smooth composite columns. Behind this facade there lies an older sixteenth-seventeenth century townhouse that once belonged to the Romieus, a prominent local family. This building now houses a gallery. O.C.

Taking the Rue Diderot along the southern side of the Hôtel de Luppé, we now come to the Rue de la Bastille on the right.

Hôtel de Donines

4, Rue de la Bastille

BUILT IN the late sixteenth century, this three-storey townhouse with an attic is a fine example of the taste for antiquity characteristic of Renaissance Provence. ALTHOUGH the ground floor and much of the first floor were altered in the eighteenth and nineteenth centuries, we can still see the fine frieze inspired by the town's Roman theatre with its triglyphs, its metopes decorated with bulls' heads and, above all, its refined rinceaus. O.C.

We now make our way back towards the end of the Rue de la Bastille, where we come to the Rue de la Calade. Here, a left turn brings us to the Roman theatre (Théâtre Antique).

Théâtre Antique

Rue de la Calade

Open: 2 Nov. - 28 Feb.
10.00–12.00, 14.00- 17.00

1 March - 30 April
9.00-12.00, 14.00-18.00

2 May - 30 Sept.: 9.00-19.00

1 Oct. - 31 Oct.
9.00-12.00, 14.00 -18.00

Along with the forum and the protective walls, the Roman theatre is one of the major constructions from the first phase of urban development in Arles. Work began in around 40-30 BC, just after the beginnings of Roman colonisation, and the structure was more or less finished by 12 BC. The building was put up along a secondary road in line with the forum, at the top of the Hauture hill.

The ruins of the Roman theatre. Below: a watercolour of the theatre by François Huard, c. 1850.

A theatre for 10 000 spectators

The *cavea* (spectators' area), has a diameter of 102 metres, making it almost identical size to the one at Orange. It rests on a system of concentric galleries, outward-radiating vaulted chambers and stairways serving the three levels which correspond to the three rows of arcades seen from the outside. Each row comprised 27 arcades.

The entrances for the public and the portico were integrated into the ground floor arcades.

ALTHOUGH a great deal of the building has been destroyed, the "Tour de Roland" can give us a good idea of its original height. This span, which overarched one of the main doorways (the second was on the northern side) has survived as a result of its inclusion in the protective wall built around the town in the fifth century.

THIS TOWER also gives us an idea of the theatre's decoration. The openings are punctuated by Doric pilasters, themselves surmounted by an entablature comprising an architrave of triglyphs (grooved stone) and metopes (carved panels), a frieze with rinceaus and a cornice. On the ground floor, which can also be seen on the north side, the metopes alternate rose and squatting bull motifs. The frieze features Cupids, birds and animals. The metopes on the first floor are adorned with roses and bulls' heads adorned with garlands for sacrifice. The second floor repeats these motifs, but on a smaller scale and with reduced ornamentation. An attic completed the elevation.

ON THE INSIDE the *cavea* comprised 33 tiers of seating forming three *maenianа* (horizontal sections). It seated 10,000. Spectators were organised by class. Plebeians sat in the upper and middle areas, the equestrian order in the lower tiers and notables in the *orchestra,* where they had moveable seats. All we have from Roman times is six rows of seats. The rest was partially rebuilt in the nineteenth century. We can make out five radiating stairways, which subdivided the *cavea* into *cunei.*

THE *BALTEUS*, a low wall separating the *cavea* from the *orchestra,* stood at the bottom of the tiers, as can be seen from signs of embedding. A gutter visible below evacuated rainwater. The *orchestra* was where the chorus performed. Elements of the original floor are still visible here, with green cipolin (onion marble) framed by pink breccia. In the centre, a hole marks the emplacement of an altar to Apollo. Two palms and two swans symbolise the god as he was celebrated on Delos.

The stage of the Roman theatre

TWO STAIRCASES gave access to the stage. The boundary was marked by the *pulpitum,* a low wall between the orchestra and the stage area proper, of which there remain only two layers of stone. This wall contained a series of circular and square recesses and was decorated with a second altar to Apollo on which, this time, the god bore the attributes traditionally given to him at Delphi: a footrest and bays. The head of this god figure could be removed, no doubt so that it could be flatteringly endowed with the features of the ruler of the day. Augustus was the first emperor to place his reign under the protection of Apollo. In doing so he sought to make it understood that a new golden age had come. On either side of this altar stood two smaller altars adorned with a civic crown (an allusion to Augustus) and two Silenus figures lying on water skins that serve as fountains. Every detail was designed to exalt the ruler and benefactor of the city and the god under whose protection he had placed himself.

The ruins seen from the Jardin d'Été.

TO THE REAR, a narrow cavity held the stage curtain, which was stowed below the floor during performances. We can still see the stone sockets for the wooden apparatus used to slide the armature that supported this curtain. The machinery was activated by a counterweight.

THE *PROSCAENIUM* –or stage proper– was six metres deep and more than fifty metres wide. The floor, whose height is indicated by a groove that is still visible at the level of the stage wall, rested on trestles. On either side there were adjacent rooms, the *parascaenia,* which provided access to the stage.

THE *FRONS SCAENAE*, in other words the wall at the back of the stage, which closed off the space on the western side, comprised some hundred columns organised over three levels. All that remains of this now are two Corinthian columns supporting a fragment of entablature. They reflect the variety of marbles and breccias used here and the polychrome treatment no doubt applied to the structure as a whole. The ground floor columns resting on a stylobate (a course of masonry) were placed in such a way as to allow room for them to be used by the actors. In the centre of this colonnade, the royal doorway was emphasised by a protruding section. Above it, a niche contained a statue of Augustus standing, as a heroic nude. This is kept at the Musée de l'Arles Antique, as are most of the pieces found on this site. It was most probably made by an important workshop in the service of the emperor and may date from the end of Augustus' reign. The body, which is in marble, contrasts with the limestone drapery, which, it seems fair to suppose, may well have been painted.

THE RECESSES that alternate with the columns along the stage wall contained sculptures made after Greek models. Among the pieces to have come down to us are some *Dancers,* which still have some of their original polychrome finish, and, above all, the *"Venus of Arles"*, which is now kept at the Louvre. Behind the stage wall there was another big wall which supported a canopy-like roof that protected the stage from rain. At the sides, this canopy was supported by the *parascaenia.*

From Roman times to excavation of the ruins

ON FEAST DAYS the theatre was the setting for numerous performances in honour of the gods. At such times tragedies, comedies, mimes and pantomimes were all put on for free. The theatre had a long career, and it is known that Emperor Constans ordered a performance here when he came to Arles in 353.

LITTLE IS KNOWN about how the theatre was destroyed. The southern part was no doubt modified in the fifth century by the addition of a defensive wall. An account of a miracle attributed to St Hilary, Bishop of Arles, in around

Model of the Roman theatre (Musée de l'Arles Antique).

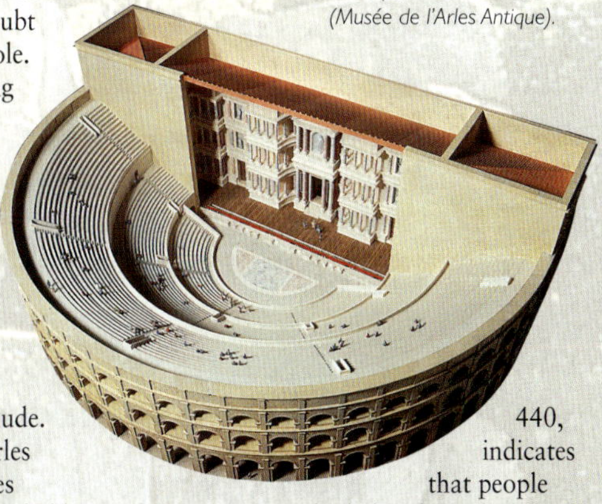

440, indicates that people had already started to remove the marble plaques from the upper part of the stage. However, come the following century St Caesarius was still decrying those who attended the city's theatre. No doubt the theatre was dismantled gradually, following the rhythm of construction work elsewhere. The first "parasitical" church known to have been built on the site was Saint-Georges, in the tenth century. In 1664, much of the area was occupied by the Couvent de la Miséricorde, which convent had taken over from a Jesuit college. The two surviving columns could be seen in its courtyard. From a watercolour by Tassy at the Museon Arlaten we know that a collection consisting of the various sculptures found on the site was presented to the public in 1788-1789. In 1833, after ten years of archaeological exploration, not to mention the prodigious clearance of the amphitheatre, work began on exhuming the vestiges of the theatre.
A.C.

1

Couvent des Franciscains *or* Couvent des Cordeliers
Collège Saint-Charles

2, Rue de la Calade

THE MENDICANT friars came to Arles in around 1218. They lived in the popular quarters of the Vieux-Bourg and Trinquetaille before settling behind the city walls in 1359. Their convent was laid out around the Rocher d'Arles. Today, all that is left is the bell-tower and the vestiges of the cloister. The church was consecrated in 1445 and rebuilt between 1716 and 1719. It has the only Gothic-style spire still to be seen in Arles, constructed by Pierre de la Chapelle. It is similar to the towers that went up in Avignon under the papacy in the fourteenth century. This bell-tower was restored in 1998 by Alain-Charles Perrot, an architect at the French department of historical monuments. The convent was sold in 1791 and served as a quarry for other buildings. The site was later occupied by the Black Penitents (1818-1830) andthe Brotherhood of the Sacred Heart of Issoudun (1875-1880). In 1884, the Sisters of Saint-Charles, an order from Lyon, had a new boarding establishment built here by the local architect Auguste Véran.The Sisters left Arles in 1978 but still own the property and have begun to restore it. A.B.

2

Chapelle des Pénitents-Gris

Rond-Point des Arènes

THE CHAPEL of the Grey Penitents stands alongside the eastern end of the Franciscan convent. The Grey Penitents were a charitable confraternity of local notables founded in 1549 and placed under the name of the Holy Cross. The chapel, whose door opens out towards the Roman amphitheatre, still has two rib-vaulted bays with painting work from circa 1665. Figures of saints (St Michael, St James the Greater, St Stephen, St Philip and St Catherine of Siena) are surmounted by a frieze bearing some words from the *Lord's Prayer*. These figures are surrounded by scenes from the Old and New Testaments. The paintings here are characteristic of the decorative vocabulary that accompanied the Counter-Reformation. A.B.

Going back down the same street, at the intersection of the Rue de la Bastille and the Rue de la Calade, we come to the Hôtel Courtois de Langlade.

Hôtel Courtois de Langlade
Sub-Prefecture

6, Rue de la Calade

THIS TOWNHOUSE goes back to the sixteenth century. In 1730 it was acquired by the Perrin family, who set about major renovation work, including the complete rebuilding of the facade in 1737. The Courtois de Langlade family became its owners in the nineteenth century. The building was converted

3

4

5

1. Bell-tower of the Couvent des Franciscains.
2. Chapelle des Pénitents-Gris.
3. Hôtel Courtois de Langlade.
4. Hôtel de Cays.
5. Hôtel Bouchaud de Bussy.

into a sub-prefecture at the turn of the following century. The external decoration bears witness to the Parisian influence on the townhouses in and around Arles in the eighteenth century. This is evident in the refinement of the Rocaille style sculptures on the facade, the small baskets or heads set at the top of the window arches and the pediment on the first floor decorated with a shell and horns of plenty.
THE INTERIOR has been much transformed since the Courtois de Langlade moved here in the nineteenth century. However, the eighteenth-century staircase is still here, as are the large salons of the piano nobile. O.C.

Just opposite, at the corner of the Rue de la Calade and the Rue du Cloître, stands the other sub-prefectural building, formerly known as the Hôtel de Cays.

Hôtel de Cays
Administrative Offices of the Sub-Prefecture

2, Rue du Cloître

THIS TOWNHOUSE belonged to one of Arles' oldest families, the Cays. A good many of its members were Consuls, Knights of Malta and outstanding soldiers. On record since the sixteenth century, this three-storey construction was renovated several times before the building work begun in 1786 erased all trace of previous transformations. The mansion's very pure and perfectly ordered classical facade dates from this period, providing eloquent testimony to the prevailing architectural fashions of the late eighteenth century. Inside, at one end of the building, there is a staircase from the same period. In 1983 the Hôtel de Cays was set aside for the needs of the Sub-Prefecture. O.C.

Continuing down the Rue de la Calade, we see on the right a hotel, the Saint-Trophime, formerly the Bouchaud de Bussy townhouse.

Hôtel Bouchaud de Bussy

16, Rue de la Calade

THIS TOWNHOUSE was bought in 1723 by Jean-François de Bouchaud de Bussy, councillor to the king at Arles. Although it still has a number of sixteenth and seventeenth-century features, its facade is a fine and highly characteristic example of the eighteenth-century Classical style with its imposing porch, the columns framing the main windows and supporting a moulded pediment, and the balanced rhythm of its openings. It is possible that the rebuilding of the facade and construction of the main staircase with its wrought iron handrail were begun shortly after Bouchaud de Bussy's arrival. The building did service as a maternity clinic between 1960 and 1980 and is now a hotel.
O.C.

A bit further on we come to the Hôtel Blain (18, Rue de la Calade) which belonged to the public prosecutor. Boasting one of the finest seventeenth-century staircases in Arles, it is now home to a book restoration centre.
At the other end of the Plan de la Cour we come to the Rue Balze.

Chapelle des Jésuites.

Chapelle des Jésuites

Rue Balze

BUILT alongside the Hôtel de Calvisson, this south-facing chapel was an integral part of the Jesuit college set up in Arles in the former Hôtel de Laval-Castellane, now occupied by the Museon Arlaten. It was built with money from a bequest by a prominent local figure, François Vaulthier, chief doctor of Queen Marie de' Medici and then to Louis XIV. The chapel was consecrated on 19 February 1961 and dedicated to St Joseph. Its main facade has a classical decorative scheme: entablatures and pronounced cornices separate the three levels, which are themselves enlivened with curvilinear or broken pediments and niches that originally contained statues. The verticality of the facade is further heightened by pilasters and columns. The interior seems unfinished because the original galleries have been replaced by large windows whose forms are nonetheless analogous to the original structure. In 1737 the ceiling was entirely redone in wood, with a flat rib vault, after a bequest from Marie de Grille d'Estoublon, the wife of Roquemartine. Her coat of arms, which can still be seen, replaced that of the first benefactors. Originally only the eastern part of the building (to the left) had side chapels. The two subsequently added along the west side were demolished in the nineteenth century.

THE ONLY furniture now left in the chapel is the high altar and the altarpiece. This "Florentine style" altar in polychrome marble with a baldachino and small columns was built in the mid-seventeenth century. The contract for the tabernacle was agreed before the notary Brunet in 1655 at a price of 1,000 livres, the parties being the master sculptor and gilder Bernable Vuezier from Forcalquier and Père André Gérard, the rector of the college. The contract for the altarpiece was awarded to Antoine Guibert in 1679. Commissioned from Louis Parrocel, an artist from Avignon, in 1691, its centrepiece was a painting of *St Joseph,* which was no doubt taken or destroyed during the Revolution. This work was replaced with a *Descent of the Holy Ghost among the Apostles* painted by Marguerit in 1690. The decoration of the upper part of the altarpiece was changed in 1685, with the addition of bas-reliefs illustrating the "name of Jesus in a glory cloud of angels and cherubim". In addition, paintings of *St Stanislas* (left) and *St Louis of Gonzaga* (right) were added. In 1936 this chapel became the Musée Lapidaire d'Art Païen, which it remained until its collection of ancient art was transferred to the new Musée de l'Arles Antique in 1993. M.B.

From the Chapelle des Jésuites we gain access to the crypto-porticus. A new entrance from Hôtel de Ville is planned.

Cryptoportiques

Rue Balze
Entrance via the Chapelle des Jésuites.
Open:
2 Nov. - 28 Feb. *10.00-12.00 , 14.00-17.00*
1 March - 30 April *9.00-12.00, 14.00-18.00*
2 May - 30 Sept.: 9.00-19.00
1 Oct. - 31 Oct. *9.00-12.00 ,14.00-18.00*

The cryptoportiques are simply the underground or invisible part of the old forum, which was the principal square of the Roman colony. About the forum as such we know very little. All that we have are two fragments of the 3,400 square-metre paved square. One of these is in the cellar of the Hôtel de Ville, the other in the cellar of a private house.
In addition, there are a few vestigial elements of the forum's decoration that allow us to date its construction to only a few years after the foundation of the colony in 46 BC.

Detail of a column in the cryptoportiques.

WHAT MADE the great Roman forum of Arles with its four monumental porticoes particularly original was the existence of these foundations, which were built to stabilise this sweeping esplanade on what was naturally sloping land. These comprise three galleries forming a U shape with its open end pointing eastwards.
Each gallery is divided in two by rectangular pillars linked by depressed arches. These galleries are known collectively as the cryptoportiques, or crypto-porticus.

Construction and transformation of the galleries

THE SOUTHERN gallery was carved out of the rock whereas the need for several metres of infilling to make the northern gallery made it possible to preserve vestiges of the pre-Roman city. These two galleries are both 90 metres long, whereas the western gallery is 60 metres long. They are just under 10 metres across at their widest. The floor level we see today is fairly close to the Roman one, when the surface was probably made of packed earth.
The galleries were ventilated and lit by airholes. The abundant light these provided can no longer be appreciated today because the gallery floors are now

more than 6 metres below pavement level. The position of the entrances and the absence of a direct connection between the galleries and the forum tend to suggest that these passages were never open to the public.

SOUTHERN GALLERY. – The southern gallery has two openings in its outer wall which mark the structure's axis of symmetry. Elsewhere the wall is blind, no doubt because of the presence of other edifices of which there remains, near the present entrance, a fairly simple mosaic that gives us an idea of where the ground level was in Roman times. In the middle of this gallery, a barrier on the inward side protects vestiges which were long thought to be the remains of a wooden floor. However, a recent study has shown that there was once a wood store here that can be dated to the early fifth century. At the end of this gallery there is a breach in the wall which was made to check the possible existence of a fourth gallery. This breach is right under the town hall, which means that it is possible to look up through the air shaft to the old prisons.

WEST GALLERY. – The west gallery, facing the present-day entrance, was lit from both sides. In fact, to the west there lay another square whose ground level was some two metres above that of the subterranean galleries. The rectangular exhedra in the centre of the west wall no doubt supported the steps leading down from the portico of the forum to this secondary square whose imposing remains can be seen in the courtyard of the Museon Arlaten.

Above: gallery under the forum. Below: cross section of the cryptoportiques, north-south axis.

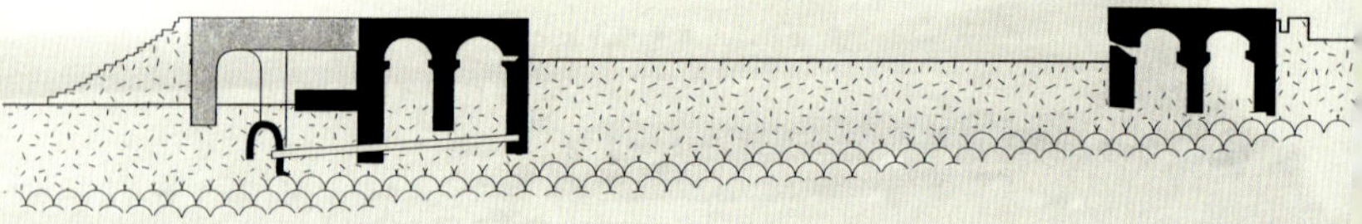

NORTHERN GALLERY. – The north gallery, which has been substantially modified, is more complex. Because of the sloping ground, it was not buried like the others but instead gave onto a square, the ancestor of today's Place du Forum. Two relatively small entrances gave access to the gallery. They flanked a row of eleven shops set into its outer wall. At the back of one of these shops we can still see the walls from the proto-historical period. The first change was made between the end of the first and the beginning of the second century, when a rectangular edifice was built in the middle of the gallery, cutting it into two unconnected parts. At the same time, this building –probably a small temple giving onto the forum– encroached on the three central shops at the northern end. Breaches made in the wall of this temple in modern times gave access to the northern end of the gallery where a store of marble was discovered in 1951. Among the items found here was a votive inscription to the Emperor Augustus and a fine marble portrait, probably of his grandson Gaius Caesar, along with other fragments of statuary, inscriptions and decorative architectural elements. For many years it was thought that this was where pagans used to hide the objects of their emperor cult from the early Christians. However, it was more probably a lime kiln that was operational in the early fifth century, which is when people began to pillage the Roman forum.

A forth gallery from late antiquity

ALTHOUGH, strictly speaking, it is not really part of the crypto-porticus, there is a fourth passage that runs parallel to the north gallery. Notable for its brick walls and vaults, it was built in late antiquity when the whole city centre was being restructured. It ran alongside the shops of the Augustan period.
In fact, the four shops on either side of the Roman forum's main temple were extended by a gallery with depressed vaults which opened onto a public square through large arcades which have now been blocked off.
At the other end the temple itself was extended towards the north with the construction of a new facade whose sole vestiges, two columns and half a pediment, are now embedded in a wall of the *Nord-Pinus*, a hotel overlooking today's Place du Forum.
In order to secure this new structure solid foundations were needed, as can be seen from the corridor that has been hollowed out here. Finally, during the Middle Ages an apse was built against the end of the gallery. This is the lower chapel of the Église Saint-Lucien, a parish church known to have stood here since the tenth century. M.H.

Hôtel Raynaud.

Opposite the Chapelle des Jésuites stand the Hôtel Reynaud and the Hôtel de Mandon.

Hôtel Raynaud

6, Rue Balze

IN THE eighteenth century this townhouse was occupied by one Gaspard Raynaud. While the fine three-storey facade dates from his time, other parts of the building are older. The facade itself is richly ornamented with a pediment, string courses, moulded architraves, garlands and pilasters.
THE HÔTEL Raynaud was also inhabited by the painter Paul Balze (1815-1884), a student of Ingres, whose frescoes can be seen at the Louvre, in the church of Saint-Symphorien at Versailles and (a collaboration with his brother) in the dome of the Galerie Dorée at the Banque de France in Paris. He also produced a number of decorative works using enamelled paint, notably the Amédée-Pichot fountain in Arles. O.C.

Hôtel de Mandon

8, Rue Balze

THIS TOWNHOUSE has been the property of two local families: the Mandons and the Eyminis. It is more discreet than is neighbour, the Hôtel Raynaud, and was partially rebuilt in the classical style in the eighteenth century. However, some of the sixteenth and seventeenth-century features remain. This three-storey building has a fine decorative porch and, on the upper level, two Corinthian pilasters resting on a sculpted keystone. O.C.

Le Rhône
Voie express
Quai de la Roquette
Tour de l'Ecorchoir
Pavillon du Canal
Chemin de Barriol
RN 113
Avenue Sixte Quenin
Marseille
Boulevard Georges Clemenceau
Boulevard des Lices
Rue Gambetta
Rue de la République
Espace Van Gogh Médiathèque
Théâtre Municipal
Museon Arlaten
Mairie
Place de la République
Eglise Saint Trophime
Cloître
Théâtre Antique
Amphithéâtre
Place du Forum
Place Antonelle
Place Patrat
Eglise St Césaire
Temple Protestant
Rue de la Calade
Rue de l'Hôtel de Ville
Sous Préfecture
Collège St.Charles
Place Bornier
Rond point des Arènes
Place de la Major
Eglise Notre Dame de la Major
Médiapôle Saint-Césaire
Tour des Mourgues
Cimetière
Boulevard Emile Combes
Rue Portagnel
Poste
Maison des Associations
Police Gendarmerie
Hôtel des Impôts
Sécurité Sociale
C.A.F.
Maison de retraite Jeanne Calment
Avenue des Alyscamps
Avenue Victor Hugo
Les Alyscamps
Ateliers S.N.C.F.
Chemin des Minimes
Chemin des Murailettes
Bourse du Travail
ANPE Formation
C.E.S Ampère
Rue Emile Zola
Rue Emile Fassin
Boulevard Alphonse Daudet
Lycée Pasquet
Boulevard Georges Marcellin
Rue Berthelot
Rue Jacquemin
Avenue du Général Leclerc
Rue Gauthier
Avenue Sadi Carnot
Rue Parmentier
Rue Etienne
Rue Couturier
Rue Casanova
Rue Lakanal
Place F.Roosevelt
Avenue de Bigot
Rue Victor Basch
Rue Antoine Talon
Centre de Secours
Avenue de la 1ère Division Française Libre
Avenue Bachaga Boualem
Rue A.France
Rue Pasteur
Rue Voltaire
Rue Constantin
EDF
Rue Mireille

From the Place Voltaire to the Espace Van Gogh

The Ramparts tour

1

2

1. Les Alyscamps.
2. Église Notre-Dame-de-la-Major: St George slaying the dragon.

The tour follows the old city walls and gives the visitor a clearer idea of what the city was like before the radical changes it underwent in the nineteenth and twentieth centuries. From the top of the hill we can see as far as the Mouleyrès district, once the site of the city's many windmills, and the Crau plain. Dotted with churches and convents all along the way, this is a journey to the heart of the religious world of the Middle Ages and the present day. The final segment takes us to the celebrated Alyscamps and the Boulevard des Lices, a lively thoroughfare that serves as a link between many of the city's focal points.

The Place Voltaire is situated in the La Cavalerie district, north of the city's conservation zone, and marks the meeting point between the old urban fabric and the area inside the walls that was rebuilt after the Second World War bombings of 1944.

IN ANCIENT TIMES what is now the Place Voltaire was the site of a triumphal arch whose demolition can be dated to the late Middle Ages. The arch gave its name to the Saint-Esprit-de-la-Cité hospital, also known as the Arc Admirable hospital, which first appears in the records in the thirteenth century.

THIS NEIGHBOURHOOD is also home to the memory of Vincent Van Gogh who, on his arrival in Arles, moved into the nearby Carrel boarding house.

Here we take the Rue Augustin-Tardieu, lined with seventeenth and eighteenth century houses. On the left we pass a modernised building into which has been incorporated the handsome gateway of the Couvent Saint-Paul.

Couvent Saint-Paul

Rue Augustin-Tardieu

ALL THAT REMAINS of the Couvent Saint-Paul is its handsome stone gateway, now part of a much more recent building. The convent was built in 1634 by the Sisters of Our Lady of Charity of the Refuge as a home for young women in difficulty. It was razed at the time of the French Revolution. O.C.

1

2

1. The Presentation in the Temple, painting on the altarpiece, Notre-Dame-de-la-Major.
2. Église Notre-Dame-de-la-Major.

As we follow the wall of the amphitheatre along to the left, it is interesting to note the two blocked-off arcades, a reminder of the Middle Ages when this Roman building served as a fortress. Next, the charming little Rue Renan (formerly Rue des Baptêmes) leads us into the Place de la Major.

Place de la Major

THE PLACE de la Major overlooks the city from the top of the L'Hauture hill, all of 25 metres above sea-level. Just a few steps from the facade of the church of Notre-Dame-de-la-Major stands an ancient column set up in honour of two famous "Félibres" ("learned men") of the Camargue: Folco de Baroncelli (1869-1943) who, with Frédéric Mistral (1830-1914) founded the newspaper *L'Aïoli,* official organ of the Félibrige movement in its struggle for a Provençal-language renaissance; and Joseph d'Arbaud (1874-1950), author of *La Bête du Vaccarès.*

A TERRACE bearing a stone engraved to the memory of d'Arbaud provides a view across the roofs of Arles to the mountains of the Alpilles, the Crau plain and, on clear days, the majestic Mont Ventoux.

THE PLACE de la Major, much larger today than in medieval times, was for a long time a necropolis. It was originally situated at the centre of a parish inhabited mainly by shepherds, small farmers and tradesmen whose little stone houses can still be seen in the neighbourhood.

The Allied bombings of 1944 damaged the church and destroyed several homes. O.C.

Église Notre-Dame-de-la-Major

Place de la Major

GIVEN THE STATUS of a collegiate chapter in 1551, the Notre-Dame-de-la-Major priory was long the centre of Arles' largest parish. Suppressed in 1791, then re-established under the Concordat of 1801, Notre-Dame was for many years home to the Brotherhood of St Véran, the patron saint of shepherds, and to a relic of St Mark which was the focal point of a solemn celebration on 25 April every year. Since the nineteenth century Notre-Dame has also been the church of the Brotherhood of Camargue Herdsmen (the famous gardians), founded in 1512 under the patronage of St George, whose statue is still in the church. On 1 May the herdsmen make a pilgrimage to Notre-Dame and have their horses blessed.

THE CHURCH of Notre-Dame-de-la-Major was built in the second half of the twelfth century on a site that may have been occupied in ancient times by a pagan temple. The evidence for this is the unearthing of an altar dedicated to Cybele, the "Great Mother", now to be found in the Musée de l'Arles Antique. This Romanesque church still has its three-bayed nave, whose barrel vault is supported by projecting jambs resting on massive piers. The semicircular apse was once adorned with eight basalt and porphyry columns, which were presented to Catherine de Médicis when she visited Arles in 1569; however they were lost when the ship transporting them sank in the Rhône.

THE CHEVET, rebuilt in the late sixteenth century, includes a cross-rib vaulted choir

1. Interior of the Église Notre-Dame-de-la-Major.
2. Église de la Madeleine.

bay and pentagonal apse, both as high as the nave. In the sixteenth century Gothic-style side-chapels began to be added to the nave, firstly on the north side and in the following century on the south. The facade as we see it now preserves all the sober elegance of the Louis XIII style. THE BELL-TOWER had been rebuilt in 1579 and was modified in the nineteenth century. Square in shape, it was topped with a pyramid to which a statue of the Virgin, designed by Lassale and executed by Cusson, was added in 1867. Cast in 1534, the bell is the oldest in the city. It was previously located at the Plan de la Cour, where it was used to summon the population to public hearings and –its main function– to sound the death knell for condemned criminals. It tolled there for the last time in 1820 and was moved to Notre-Dame-de-la-Major in 1870.
AMONG THE FURNISHINGS in the church are a polychrome marble pulpit in the style of Emmanuel Cavalho, from the second half of the eighteenth century, and a gilt wooden altar brought here from the church of Saint-Blaise. In addition to the statue of *St George* venerated by the herdsmen, there are two other statues, both commissioned in the nineteenth century: a *Sacred Heart of Jesus*, designed by Overbeck and sculpted by Hauffman, and a Virgin by the Italian sculptor Monti. There is also a wrought-iron cross originally on the Pont des Flâneurs, many crosses having been forcibly removed from public places during the anticlerical upsurge of 1901. The altarpiece in the choir bears three paintings from the first half of the eighteenth century: *The Annunciation*, *The Visitation* and *The Presentation in the Temple*. M.B.

We now take the Rue de la Madeleine, to the right. On the left an unassuming facade is a reminder of the former Église de La Madeleine (church of Mary Magdalene).

Église de la Madeleine

Rue de la Madeleine

THE ÉGLISE de la Madeleine is first referred to in the twelfth century. Initially quite small, the parish took over its neighbour, Saint-Jean-de-Moustiers in 1315 and was in turn absorbed by Notre-Dame-de-la-Major in the fifteenth century. It then became a simple chapel. Sold at the time of the Revolution, it is now private property. Totally reworked, the original facade is now scarcely visible and no trace of ornamentation remains. M.B.

Next door, the former water board offices have been occupied since 1995 by the Materials Research Laboratory (LERM), specialist in hydraulic binders. The LERM also carries out research into new types of concrete and building materials and carries out diagnostic studies for the restoration of historical monuments.

The old reservoirs

Rue de la Madeleine

THIS WAS the site chosen for the la Major reservoirs in the early twentieth century. Fed by the waterworks in the Rue du Docteur-Fanton –the establishment responsible for the city's water supply–

1

2

the reservoirs were initially in the open air. The tower that dominates the structure was built in 1960 and provides the pressure needed for supplying the L'Hauture district. The water board set up its offices here in premises built in the 1970s and remained until 1988. O.C.

Continuing along the Rue de la Madeleine, we reach the Place de la Redoute; from there the Rue Émile-Barrère leads us to the door of the Abbaye Saint-Césaire.

Abbaye Saint-Césaire
Media centre

Rue du Grand-Couvent

THE ABBEY was named after one of Arles' greatest bishops, Caesarius, who held episcopal office from 502 until his death in 542. Born c. 470 in Chalon-sur-Saône and famous for his sermons, Caesarius decided in 506 to found a monastery for women, but the first building was destroyed when the city was besieged by the Franks and the Burgundians in 507-508. After the liberation of Arles by the Visigoths, he set about rebuilding the monastery, but this time within the city walls, near the former cathedral. The monastery was consecrated in 512, its dedication to St John doubtless being a reference to the baptistry built by Arles' first bishop. The rule Caesarius laid down for the enclosed order of nuns gained enormous prestige and was adopted by other convents such as that founded in Poitiers by St Radegonde.
IN THE MIDDLE AGES the Abbaye Saint-Césaire was a substantial owner of property on the Crau plain and in the Camargue. It also had jurisdiction over a part of Les Alyscamps and the Église Saint-Césaire-le-Vieux (eleventh-twelfth century) at the entry to the necropolis there; nothing remains of the church now except the large Romanesque arcade standing next to the Chapelle Saint-Accurse.
A LARGE eighteenth-century gate marks the entry to the abbey grounds. Inside, the gatehouse in which the lay-sisters lived possesses a number of architectural features dating from the fifteenth century; these notably include basket-handle apertures, some of which have since been filled in. On the right can be seen traces of a wicket-gate and on the left the handsome staircase tower which is all that remains of the abbess' quarters. Continuing on into the garden, we see traces of a cloister, but the monastery buildings were in the main demolished after the Revolution. The convent was closed in 1792 and sold off as state property in 1793. In the late nineteenth century an old people's home was built on the site and was occupied until the 1980s. The premises have since been turned into a centre for new media and technology. O.C.

Église Saint-Blaise

Rue du Grand-Couvent

OF THE MANY CHAPELS and churches once to be found in the L'Hauture district, two are still in existence, quite close to each other: Saint-Blaise and Saint-Jean-de-Moustiers.
SAINT-BLAISE, the church for the nuns of the Abbaye Saint-Césaire, was built in several stages. The oldest part,

3

1. Abbaye Saint-Césaire: the gatehouse.
2. Église Saint-Blaise.
3. Église Saint-Jean-de-Moustiers.

containing the apse –now demolished– a transept and an initial round-arched bay, may date from the mid-twelfth century and can be identified by workers' "signatures" not to be found in buildings from the later phases.
At the end of the century a second, pointed-arch bay was added across the entire width and the division into three naves that characterised the first phase was abandoned. The north wall bears the epitaph of Abbess Eudiardis, who died in 1229. A century later the church was extended by the addition of a third bay, also with a single nave but slightly narrower. At the springing point of the vault are acoustic chambers designed to reduce echo within the nave. The main door is slightly off true north and some 150 centimetres higher than the thirteenth-century paving, an indication of just how much the floor level has been raised. In the fifteenth century a tall window was inserted above the entry.
CONVERTED to secular uses at the Revolution, the inside of the church was filled and levelled and a new floor put in; the present door must also date from this period. In more recent times the building has been used as a storehouse and a funeral parlour workshop.
The archaeological excavations carried out between 1972 and 1982 brought to light floor levels corresponding to the different phases of construction, together with remains pre-dating the Romanesque period. At the far end of the church was found a cement and broken tile floor that is certainly of great antiquity. To reach it on the western side one crossed limestone flagging surrounding a non-paved area, with columns at each corner. This pre-Romanesque feature cannot be readily explained, at least until more detailed excavations have taken place. Probes carried out here have revealed traces of pre-Roman occupation.
INSIDE THE CHURCH is to be found the lid of a sarcophagus datable to the mid-sixth century by the chrisma –the divine monogram– sculpted on its side. Found in 1945 or thereabouts under the floor of the south transept, it is believed to come from the tomb of St Caesarius, whose relics were kept here until the Revolution. M.H.

Église Saint-Jean-de-Moustiers

Rue du Grand-Couvent

FOUNDED in approximately the ninth century, the Chapelle Saint-Jean-de-Moustiers was a parish church in its own right before being incorporated into the parish of Notre-Dame-de-la-Major in 1315. Also known in Romanesque times as the Église Sainte-Agathe, Saint-Jean-de-Moustiers was took its name from the sixth century monastery of Saint-Jean, founded by St Caesarius not far from the disused baptistry of the first episcopal complex. Outside, the semi-circular apse is decorated with fluted pilasters whose acanthus-leaf capitals are topped with an overhanging cornice; the inspiration here comes directly from local Roman monuments, notably the amphitheatre. The filling-in of the apse –it is buried to half its height– is due to the raising of the floor level since the Romanesque period, something already observed in the church of Saint-Blaise. Two bays of the nave have survived, one of them partly incorporated into the

adjacent house. Two doors and a window in the north and south walls are further testimony to the change in level between the time of construction and the present day. The most noteworthy feature here is the round-arched apse, whose ribbing terminates in capitals around a central boss formerly decorated with a lamb. The apse wall is decorated with partially restored arcatures. M.H.

Retracing our steps, we come to the Place de la Redoute. At the far end is the little postern that juts out over the Boulevard Émile-Combes, a medieval opening added to the Augustan rampart. The part of the rampart to the left of it was modified in the Middle Ages and named Château de la Redoute. To the right we note the facing on the inside of the rampart with, higher up, the evidence of successive reconstructions. Beyond the postern, on the left, is the Porte d'Auguste.

Porte d'Auguste

Boulevard Émile-Combes

THE PORTE d'Auguste (Augustus' Gate) –also known as the Porte de la Redoute, in reference to the fortress built there in the Middle Ages– is set at the centre of an enormous half-moon-shaped area in the eastern part of the Augustan rampart. At each end of the half-moon, which has a perimeter of some 100 metres, a circular tower ensured the connection with the facade. The gateway itself was 35 metres wide and, unlike the more summary rampart, was built entirely of large blocks of stone held together with mortar. The many alterations effected in the course of the centuries have left the gateway in fairly poor condition, only the two towers giving a real idea of the original quality of the whole. The base of each tower is decorated with the same relatively simple mouldings that are found, in a poor state of preservation, at the top. All trace of any openings has vanished. Between the two towers there is enough space for two lines of vehicles, but the 15-metre width may not have been able to accommodate two additional paths for pedestrians, as we find in the case of the slightly wider Porte d'Auguste in Nîmes (20 metres between the towers and an overall width of 39 metres).

SITUATED at the highest point in the city, the Porte d'Auguste controlled one of the major access roads, an offshoot of the Aurelian Way which itself ran from Aix to Tarascon, where it joined the Domitian Way. However, the current siting of the gate, which provides a view over the distant countryside, is due to the digging-out of the Boulevard Émile-Combes in the late eighteenth century; thus its relative position is certainly not the same as in ancient times, when the road at the top of the Mouleyrès hill climbed gently towards the Porte d'Auguste.

IN LATE antiquity or the early Middle Ages, the Porte d'Auguste was closed off by a wall of large blocks of stone, although an opening may have been retained next to the south tower.

LATER STILL –doubtless during the Middle Ages– the height of this wall was increased by the addition of smaller blocks of stone. It can fairly be supposed that the postern introduced into the facade directly south of the south tower was created at the same time. M.H.

1. Porte d'Auguste.
2. Roman aqueduct.

2

We descend the little staircase to the boulevard, originally created by cutting a large slice out of the hillside. Here, in the rock and on the other side of the road are traces of the arrival of the Roman aqueduct.

Roman aqueduct

Boulevard Émile-Combes

DESPITE its location on the banks of the Rhône, Arles was supplied with drinking water by two aqueducts linking it to the chain of the Alpilles, over 50 kilometres away. The first of these came from the northern slope of the Alpilles, bypassing them to the west and running south of the village of Fontvieille to join up with the second, shorter aqueduct which collected the runoff from the southern foothills. From here on a single aqueduct crossed the Crau plain and entered the city via a "pipe" cut into the rock near the north tower of the Porte d'Auguste. Limestone deposits are visible on the inside of the aqueduct at the point where it is cut short by the boulevard. M.H.

The cemetery

Boulevard Émile-Combes

IT TOOK the royal edict of 1776 to put a halt to burial of the dead in churches, a practice dating back to the Middle Ages. This was purely and simply a necessary public health measure. The Arles cemetery, the only surviving one of its kind in Provence, was opened in 1786; the population initially showed misgivings about the new-style burials, but Perrin de Jonquières, a member of the aristocracy, set the example, by being the first notable to opt for interment elsewhere than in the ancient family vault.
SOME of Provence's oldest nineteenth-century tombs are also to be found here. One distinctive type is a raised vault with twin stelas, of which other examples can be seen in the area around Arles.
O.C. [AFTER RÉGIS BERTRAND]

We now move on towards the nearby La Croisière crossroads, following the rampart as it leads us to the Tour des Mourgues. *Mourgues* is a Provençal word meaning "nuns belonging to enclosed orders" and refers here to the convent that once stood just behind the tower.

Tour des Mourgues and ramparts

Intersection of the Boulevard Émile-Combes and the Boulevard des Lices

LIKE MOST of the colonies founded in the late first century BC in the Roman province centred on Narbonne, Arles was ringed by an enormous rampart. The route followed by this fortification –probably intended more for show than for actual military purposes– is only partially known. On the north side of the city it can be followed from the north-eastern corner as far as the amphitheatre. Beyond this point all trace is lost, but the rampart must have continued on as far as the Rhône in the form of an assemblage of large blocks of dressed stone –stacked without mortar– dating from the first half of the century. On the south side the

Tour des Mourgues.

old walls followed what is now the southern edge of the Boulevard des Lices, but it is not known just how this section joined up with the south-east corner. All trace of the west side has been lost, but substantial remains of the walls are to be found to the east, along the Boulevard Émile-Combes. The result of the digging-out of this thoroughfare in the late eighteenth century is that today's traffic flows several metres lower than in Roman times.

AND SO it is the east side that gives us the clearest idea of the architecture of the city wall. Built here of spalled rubble –small, regularly-shaped fragments of rock– the rampart was flanked by several circular towers, of which the best-preserved is the Tour des Mourgues.

THIS TOWER has undergone various external modifications. Firstly, on its north side and doubtless in late Antiquity, the original structure was faced with recycled dressed stone. The south side was also reinforced, probably in the fourteenth century, by a sloping embankment.

HOWEVER, it is from the inside that we get the best idea of the original character of the building. With an internal diameter of almost 8 metres, it gave onto the city via a door with a curved lintel and a relieving arch, while a postern provided the link with the outside. The postern shows that the ground level at the time was the same inside and outside the city.

THE NAME Tour des Mourgues ("tower of the enclosed order of nuns") is a reference to the women's monastery of Saint-Jean, founded by Bishop Caesarius in the early sixth century. The monastery was in the south-east corner of the city, adjacent to the rampart. Just in front of the tower can be seen the remains of one of the monastery's Paleo-Christian chapels.

IMMEDIATELY to the west of the Tour des Mourgues, the outside of the rampart built during the reign of Augustus (27 BC-14 AD) was later faced with dressed stone. A square tower, modified during the Middle Ages, was also added. Near the point where the late Roman section of the wall begins, following the Montée Vauban, once stood a tower belonging to the Augustan rampart.

ALONG the eastern section, in addition to the Porte d'Auguste and its towers, there can be seen various traces of other, poorly preserved towers.

The angle tower at the north-east corner, behind the church of Notre-Dame-de-la-Major, cannot be described as Roman in its present state. There are also traces of another tower south of this one, but later modifications have made its study impossible.

REMAINS of two other towers can be seen between the north-east angle tower and the amphitheatre, whose construction necessitated the demolition of a third tower. This demolition is proof that the Augustan ramparts, then about a century old, no longer served their original function. M.H.

Crossing the la Croisière intersection, we go down the Avenue des Alyscamps to the Craponne canal, built by Adam Craponne in the sixteenth century. The canal brings water from the river Durance to the Crau plain and flows into the Rhône.

Les Alyscamps

Avenue des Alyscamps

Open: 2 November-28 February, 10:00-12:00 and 14:00-17:00

1 March-30 April, 9:00-12:00 and 14:00-18:00

2 May-30 September, 9:00-19:00

1 October-31 October, 9:00-12:00 and 14:00-18:00

While the name Les Alyscamps is associated with the Christian era and generally taken as including the Église Saint-Honorat and the avenue of sarcophagi created in the seventeenth century, it can also be taken as meaning the whole of the eastern necropolis along the Aurelian way.

RECENT studies and excavations mean we are now better informed about the development of the necropolis. Dating from the late first century BC, its oldest section was to be found right at the foot of the city wall. While this upper area was only used for the ashes of the deceased, the necropolis began to extend further down towards the south and east in the second century AD, when actual burial began to be practised.

TRADITION has it that the Arles martyr St Genesius was buried at the south-east end of the necropolis, where the Église Saint-Honorat now stands. Genesius was a clerk of the court who refused to sign death sentences during the time of the persecutions by the Emperor Decius (250 AD). Pursued by Roman legionaries, he swam across the Rhône but was apprehended at Trinquetaille and his head was cut off near a mulberry tree. His body was brought back onto the left bank and interred at Les Alyscamps in an area apparently not previously used for burials. Over the centuries these two spots became the focal points of necropolises ad sanctos ("near the saints") and Christian writers of the fifth and sixth centuries often mention that the city of Genesius, *urbs Genesii*, is protected by the martyr's body and blood. Just when Genesius began to be venerated is not known.

Sculpted head.

Top: the sarcophagi and the Église Saint-Honorat.
Above: courtyard of the Église Saint-Honorat

The tomb of Genesius is most unlikely to have stood out among the relatively few others in the area. The excavation of the crypt of Saint-Honorat brought to light a number of wood-lined tombs that can be dated to the fourth century, but none of them shows any signs of specifically religious preparation; indeed, they do not even appear to be Christian. Other graves dating from the fourth century were excavated in 1975 on the former Jardin d'Hiver ("Winter Garden") site, over 700 metres to the west, where several epitaphs indicate that these were Christian burials. Throughout most of the fourth century and in spite of the growth of Christianity, the tomb of St Genesius failed to attract any great number of elaborate burials and none of the marble-faced sarcophagi –which make up one of the most impressive collections of their kind in the world– was found near the presumed site of his grave.

IT WAS ONLY in the second half of the fourth century, a time of rising enthusiasm for relics, that the area around Genesius' grave became a coveted burial site, notably for the bishops of Arles. The first of these was doubtless Concordius, who died in about 380-390.

However, the first soundly attested funerary basilica on the site dates only from the mid-fifth century, when Bishop Hilarius was buried *"in basilica sancti Genesii"*. Excavations in the period 1930-1950 revealed an accumulation of tombs of members of the faithful wishing to lie as close as possible to the martyr and his aura of sanctity. Relatively simple and without ornament or epitaph, these sarcophagi were placed in burial enclosures that were probably family or collegiate concessions. Several such enclosures succeeded each other, although their exact chronology remains uncertain. A wall on the site yielded a shard of pottery datable to the period 360-470, –the same as indicated by coins found in much earlier excavations– in company with slightly more recent pottery remains.

THESE ENCLOSURES show a slightly different orientation in relation to the Église Saint-Honorat, built in the eleventh century to replace a pre-Romanesque church of uncertain date. In the Middle Ages the eastern part of the Les Alyscamps necropolis belonged to the powerful Abbaye Saint-Victor-de-Marseille, while the western section was part of the monastery of Saint-Jean, founded by Bishop Caesarius in the early sixth century. The name of the Arles martyr was doubtless insufficiently prestigious for the monks of Saint-Victor, who replaced it with that of St Honoratus, bishop of Arles from 426 to 429; Honoratus was known above all as founder of the monastery on the island of Lérins which, together with Saint-Victor, was one of the seminal points of Provençal monasticism.

Église Saint-Honorat

THE HISTORY of the building of the church of Saint-Honorat remains unclear. The crypt of the Romanesque structure includes an earlier apse of uncertain date, while the north side wall of the nave incorporates a dressed stone doorway that still conserves traces of twelfth-century paintings. Once thought to be the principal door of an original, north-west facing chapel, this doorway certainly antedates today's church, but is aligned with a gutter-bearing wall indicating the existence of a pre-Romanesque church on the same site. This wall and its equivalent to the south enclose the unfinished western part of the Romanesque nave, begun within the older shell somewhere about 1130-1160.

Les Alyscamps *by Paul Gauguin, 1888 (Musée d'Orsay).*

RESEARCH into changes of level and an archaeological probe have provided a useful overview of the long and doubtless highly complex evolution of this building. The initial phase included spalled rubble walls whose round-arch window frames, angles and north-western gateway were made with dressed stone apparently obtained by re-using sarcophagi. The facade of this initial nave was already in place on the site of the twelfth-century facade. During the second phase, in all probability subsequent to the taking-over of the church by the monks of Saint-Victor in 1040-1044, the building was extended westwards, its height increased and new south windows added. Of this second structure there basically remains only the south wall, which still bears traces of the toothing of the facade. In the second half of the twelfth century it was decided to rebuild the church while retaining the walls of the first nave. Made entirely of dressed stone, the building included a chevet with three apses and a small choir bay giving onto a transept.

THE CRYPT under the enormous, raised main apse housed relics of St Genesius, St Honoratus and other bishop-saints of early Christian times. Initially it could only be reached via two long side corridors. Above the crossing rises a dome set on squinches, surmounted by a fine two-storey octagonal bell-tower whose decoration shows signs of Roman influence. In the sixteenth century the transept was modified by the introduction of cylindrical blocks designed to reinforce the Romanesque pillars and by dividing each existing arcade in two.

THE TRIPLE NAVE, with its barrel vaults all springing at the same height, was never brought to completion. Only the last of the five planned bays and the south wall of the fourth were built, together with the bases of some of the pillars and the beginning of the west facade. The latter has a handsome great door in the late twelfth-century Romanesque style. According to contemporary records building came to a halt in the early thirteenth century, but there were additions in the form of funerary niches cut into the walls. Numerous funerary chapels, now partially in ruins, were grafted onto the venerable church between the fifteenth and seventeenth centuries.

Église Saint-Honorat.

Inside the church.

The Les Alyscamps chapels

LES ALYSCAMPS are the subject of many legends, one of which has it that because of a miraculous current in the Rhône, the bodies of those wishing to be buried near the holy relics preserved in the crypt of the Église Saint-Honorat were washed up on a sandy beach near the city. A chanson de geste relates that the sarcophagi on the site had risen up out of the ground to receive the bodies of those killed in a battle between Charlemagne and the Saracens. The many pilgrims undertaking thepilgrimage to Saint James of Compostella came here to think on first and last things, and helped spread the legends.

THE SITE was once home to a host of funerary chapels, all of them now destroyed except those of Saint-Accurse and the Porcelets, and those –the Mollèges and Oraison family chapels (fifteenth and seventeenth centuries respectively)– built onto the Église Saint-Honorat.

CHAPELLE SAINT-ACCURSE. – Situated at the entry to the site, it was originally built onto the church of Saint-Césaire-le-Vieux, of which only the Romanesque porch has survived. The chapel was built in 1520 to atone for the death of Accurse de la Tour, killed in a duel with Antoine de Quiqueran; both were young Arlesian nobles.

CHAPELLE DE LA FAMILLE DES PORCELETS. – Just beyond the chapel of Saint-Accurse, on the left, lies the fifteenth-century chapel of the Porcelet ("Piglet") family. Legend has it that the family owed its name to a woman beggar who, jostled in the street by a lady, put a curse on her: she would give birth on a single occasion to children as numerous as the litter of a local sow.

The decline of Les Alyscamps

IN SPITE of the late modifications to the Église Saint-Honorat, Les Alyscamps were already in a state of semi-abandonment when the necropolis was encroached on by the Craponne canal in the sixteenth century.

IN 1616 the Friars Minim took over the site, building a monastery and creating its avenues of sarcophagi.

It was then that the archbishops of Arles began to take measures to prevent the constant pillaging of the tombs there, but this protection was to last only two centuries.

LAID WASTE during the Revolution, the ancient burial ground was partially obliterated by the passage of the Paris-Lyon-Mediterranean railway line, then definitively devastated by the building of the railway workshops in the mid-nineteenth century.

M.H. - A.H.-V.

Monument to Vincent Van Gogh in the Jardin d'Été. Bronze by William Earl Singer (1969).

Retracing our footsteps along the Avenue des Alyscamps, we come to the Boulevard des Lices. The city's main thoroughfare, the boulevard is particularly famous for its Saturday morning market. Situated outside the ramparts, it was lined with necropolises in Roman times before becoming a venue for tourneys in the Middle Ages. Systematic planning and tree-planting began in the eighteenth century and the boulevard became a favourite strolling spot for the people of Arles.

Jardin public or Jardin d'Été

Boulevard des Lices

Open

Summer: 7:30-20:00

Winter: 7:30-18:00

JARDIN D'ÉTÉ: a name that conjures up all the delightful coolness of its summer shade and a total contrast with the former Jardin d'Hiver ("Winter Garden"). Until 1976 the latter was a series of sun-splashed terraces on the other side of the boulevard, a true French-style formal garden that has since surrendered its site to a parking lot.

THE BOULEVARD des Lices offers a panoramic view of the Jardin d'Été against the backdrop of the Théâtre Antique. Laid out in 1864, the garden was created by the municipality to set off that building in a tribute to the Antiquity so dear to the Romantic period. Set at the foot of the medieval rampart that once enclosed the southern wall of the Théâtre, its islands of greenery are home to such exotics as the Japanese gingko, cedars from the Atlas mountains and magnolias from Asia, all of which mingle harmoniously with more local species like the nettle tree, also known as the "elephant tree" from the shape of the base of its trunk, its colour and the "wrinkles" where its branches begin.

THE GINGKO, of course, is Japan's emblematic tree. In 1853 that country had just opened its frontiers after two centuries of self-sufficiency, flooding the West with the products of an entirely different culture. The garden is host to three gingkos, one male and two females: the latter can be identified by their fruit –ovules, to be more exact– which are the size of apricots but give off a nauseating smell when they fall in autumn. The choice of the gingko was perhaps the sign of an urge to modernity; they were described at the time as "living fossils", their presence going back to the Jurassic. In autumn the distinctive leaves –each one a fusion of many needles– turn gold, whence the further nickname of "the gold coin tree". Another curious feature of the garden is a gingko branch that has twisted out of shape to avoid contact with a fir tree.

IN THE HEART of the garden is a pond with, at its centre, a statue of *Niobe*, daughter of Tantalus, created by the sculptor Hippolyte Lefebvre in 1897. Continuing downhill, we see on the left a bronze relief of Vincent Van Gogh by the American sculptor William Earl Singer, who made a gift of it to the City in 1969. From this point we see, peeping above the greenery, a fine fifteenth-century hexagonal tower with its little bartizan or battlemented tower. Once part of the canon's estate, the tower became a school in the nineteenth century and now belongs to the City. CATH.S.

1

2

Opposite the Summer Garden is the memorial to the dead of two World Wars. The base was designed by the architect J.-A. Gibert in 1930, while Gaston de Luppé modelled the bronze statue of a woman brandishing the crown of martyrdom and the stone design on the base showing the lion of Arles surrounded by coats of arms. A little further along on the left we see the *Hôtel Jules-César* and the Chapelle de la Charité, once the Couvent des Carmélites.

Couvent des Carmélites

Boulevard des Lices

THE CARMELITE order of nuns came to Arles in 1631 and on 3 June 1634 acquired an enclosed plot of land near the Porte du Marché-Neuf for a monastery and chapel. The land in question lay between the paupers' cemetery and the nearby Hôpital de la Charité. As happened to so many other religious communities, the Revolution resulted in the Carmelites' being expelled and, in this case, their monastery being used as new premises for the Hôpital de la Charité, whose existing building were considered too antiquated. Returning to Arles in 1823, but unable to recover their former buildings, they took over the former monastery of the Recollect friars –today the Collège Frédéric-Mistral– only to find themselves driven out again by the upsurge of anticlerical feeling that marked the late nineteenth century. Nonetheless, the early years of the twentieth century saw them back in Arles, in the new buildings in the Mouleyrès quarter where they remain to this day.

AFTER the closing of the Hôpital de la Charité, the former Carmelite convent was put up for sale on 21 March 1903. A consortium made a proposal for transforming the building into a luxury hotel, and in October 1920 the municipal council approved the scheme; however, the chapel was only handed over in 1927, on the understanding that it was to become a concert hall managed by the hotel.

WHEN work began on the project, the remains of the Carmelites buried on the site were removed from their tombs and transferred to the Mouleyrès monastery. In spite of their change of function, the buildings were carefully preserved, as was the chapel on the Boulevard des Lices. Its facade includes a porch flanked by two pairs of columns with Corinthian capitals and topped with a broad triangular pediment; the pediment is in turn set off by a curvilinear spandrel bearing a heart pierced by an arrow and set in a cloud embellished with cherubs.

WITH the notable exception of the communion table, transferred to the choir of Saint-Trophime, the chapel has retained a substantial part of its original furniture. Of special interest is the wooden pulpit, the work of Avignon sculptor Péru, who was also the creator of the Baroque main altarpiece. The focal point here is an *Apotheosis of St Theresa* painted by Pierre Parrocel of Avignon in 1718.

THE PLAN and layout of the new hotel complex were the work of the architect

1. and 2. Facade and interior of the Chapelle de la Charité, Couvent des Carmélites.
3. Hôpital de la Charité.

3

Bentz, who opted for the Provençal style. Visible from the Boulevard des Lices, the colonnade takes its inspiration from that of the municipal casino in Aix-en-Provence. We owe the murals and interior decoration to the Marseille designer Apy. The hotel opened on 22 March 1928. M.B.

Just beyond the hotel is the bandstand, erected in 1902 opposite the cafes that line the boulevard. Further along, on the left and at a lower level than the Boulevard, is a building once part of the old Hôpital de la Charité.

Hôpital de la Charité

Rue Émile-Fassin

REFLECTING the influence of the work of St Vincent de Paul, the Hôpital de la Charité was founded as a place where beggars would be lodged, fed, cared for and taught a trade.

ON 12 MARCH 1641 Monsignor de Barrault, Archbishop of Arles, called on the faithful to make contributions to the building of the hospital. Once bought, the land was blessed on 8 December 1641, but the building was only completed on 12 April 1661. On that day all the city's beggars were assembled in the courtyard of the Archbishop's palace, whence they moved in procession to the new hospital.

LIKE THE HÔTEL-DIEU hospital, the Charité was staffed by Augustine nuns. It's running was financed by gifts, legacies and public collections, as well as by the work of the poor who lived there. Built in a highly classical style, it originally had two storeys, but repeated modifications have considerably changed its appearance and only the facade of the west wing is in something approaching original condition. The central part of this wing is highlighted by a triangular pediment.

IN 1792 the Hôpital de la Charité was transferred to the former Carmelite monastery. Turned into a stud farm in 1802, the hospital became the Arles labour exchange in the twentieth century.
M.B.

Excavations carried out beside the tourist office in 1976 uncovered the extension of the *cardo*, the main north-south road of the Roman era, together with houses and baths of the same period. This is the perfect starting point for an exploration of the Chabourlet quarter and its Art Deco houses, south of the Boulevard des Lices. Simply turn left down the Rue Émile-Zola, then left again along the Rue du Commandant-L'Herminier, returning via the Rue Émile-Fassin.

Chabourlet quarter

EXCEPT for its northern fringe, known to have been inhabited since Roman times, the Chabourlet quarter –marked out by the Craponne canal to the north and the Vigueirat canal to the south– remained rural and, in parts, marshy until the late nineteenth century. It only really began to take shape in the early twentieth century, during a period of widespread expansion of the city beyond its walls. This trend was mainly the work of property developers taking advantage of the breakup of large

properties and transforming them into housing estates.

UNDER the terms of the "Loucheur law" of 1928, fifty-year loans could be made available to potential homebuyers. This led to a new kind of urban habitat and, in the 1930s, a proliferation of detached houses for an emergent bourgeoisie.

THESE HOUSES were set side by side, each having a garden that was a kind of miniature park, with an iron gate and sumptuous plants of which palm trees and magnolias were among the most popular. Built of Fontvieille stone, they were as a rule ornamented with Provençal motifs or such fashionable modernities as friezes of glazed tiles bearing flower and plant designs. Most of the city's public buildings date from this period, but private-sector building continued on until the end of the 1960s. S.R.

Further along the Boulevard des Lices, on the right, stands a tall building that is now a Protestant place of worship. Entry is by a double staircase.

La Rotonde
Protestant church

Rue de la Rotonde

LA ROTONDE is the only substantial building in Arles dating from the time of the Revolution. Designed to house a club –or gambling circle– it was built in 1790 for the Arles notables, who held dances and parties there. Nîmes architect Loizon the Younger opted for a symmetrical structure based around a single central point, using a neo-classical style reminiscent of that of Claude Nicolas Ledoux, designer of the saltworks at Arc-et-Senans and the gates of Paris.

THE ROTUNDA itself was an enormous, circular room with a low vault and was decorated with a cornice wide enough for lamps to stand on. It opened onto the esplanade, on the south side. During the revolutionary turmoil that began in 1792, the building went through many trials and tribulations before finally being acquired by the Reformed Church of France in the nineteenth century.

THE INTERIOR can only be inspected on Sunday mornings, at the time of the weekly service. O.C.

Continuing down the boulevard and crossing the Rue Gambetta, we reach the Théâtre Municipal.

Théâtre municipal

Boulevard des Lices

BEFORE the Revolution, plays were performed in the former real tennis court near the Théâtre Antique.

Two meeting rooms –the Waux-Hall, built in 1760 on what is now the Rue Jean-Jaurès and demolished in 1793, and La Rotonde, built in 1790– also served for a time as gaming rooms and theatres.

IN 1828, the municipal council decided to built a proper theatre and concert hall, and compulsorily acquired the

2

3

1. La Rotonde (Protestant church).
2, 3. Théâtre Municipal (details).
4. Espace Van Gogh, formerly the Hôtel-Dieu hospital.

4

houses on the proposed site. However, the scheme was delayed by the host of problems that followed –demolitions, planning improvements to the surrounding area (the Boulevard Gambetta only came into being in the 1880s), alignment problems and the choosing of the appropriate project– with the result that it was 1837 before plans by the architect Bourdon were approved and work actually got under way.

TO ALL INTENTS and purposes this is a small Italian-style theatre with seating for around five hundred, but its eclectic design makes it pure mid-nineteenth century.

THE FACADE is neoclassical with a tinge of Mannerism added by masks and mascarons.

IN 1902 THE CITY had a fashionable terrace added, complete with metal railing and cast-iron pillars.

IN 1951 the building's general state of dilapidation made improvements imperative; but even so, and after being closed for several years, it was only in 2001 that a thoroughly renovated Théâtre Municipal was once again opened to the public.

O.C.

To the right of the theatre, at the very beginning of the Rue Gambetta, is the Rue Molière.

We turn here and follow the facade of the former Hôtel-Dieu hospital, now the Espace Van Gogh, for fifty metres or so; a striking feature of the building is the minimal number of windows, the theory of the time being that the spread of illness could be prevented by shutting the sick away. A short staircase on the left leads to the entry.

Espace Van Gogh Formerly the Hôtel-Dieu Saint-Esprit

Rue du Président-Wilson

Multimedia Library

Place Félix-Rey

Tel. 04.90.49.39.39

Fax 04.90.93.80.85

E-mail: mediatheque@ville-arles.fr

Website: www.ville-arles.fr

Opening times:

Tuesday to Friday 13:00-18:30

Saturday 10:00-12:00 and 13:00-17:00

Municipal archives

Opening times:

Tuesday, Thursday and Friday 13:30-17:00

Wednesday 9:00-12:00 and 13:30-17:00

Saturday 9:00-12:00

THE ESPACE VAN GOGH is now home to the multimedia library (Médiathèque), the municipal archives, the literary translators' college and the University of Arles.

FOUNDED in the 16th century by Archbishop Jean Ferrier, the Hôtel-Dieu Saint-Esprit united all of the city's thirty-two charitable institutions on one spot in the Marché-Neuf quarter. In the Middle Ages, this was the site of the market (it was later moved to the square in front of the town hall, today's Place de la République, and, much later, to the Boulevard des Lices). Home to

2

1

1. Espace Van Gogh: inner courtyard.
2. Interior of the Hôtel-Dieu by Van Gogh (Winterthur Museum).
3. Multimedia library.

the city's inns, the Marché-Neuf quarter was close to the handsome city gate of the same name, regrettably demolished in the late nineteenth century.

THE FIRST stone of the Hôtel-Dieu Saint-Esprit hospital was laid on 24 February 1573. The hospital was open to the city's sick, abandoned children under seven, orphans and children whose parents were ill or impoverished. The generosity of its middle-class and noble patrons had provided the Hôtel-Dieu with land in the Camargue and houses in the city itself, all of which brought in useful income. In addition there were gifts, backing from the City, the revenue accruing from church collections and the property of those who died leaving no family. Even so, the hospital's rectors regularly had to raise loans to cover everyday running costs.

COMPRISED of lay people and members of religious orders, the staff also included a treasurer, a bursar, a porter, a baker and various servants. Among the medical and educational personnel were doctors, two surgeons, an apothecary and women supervisors for the orphans and young children. Two priests ministered to the sick and celebrated the last rites. From 1664 onwards the sick were looked after by the nuns hospitallers of the Augustine order.

CONSTRUCTION of the Hôtel-Dieu took two centuries, the buildings forming a rectangle around a garden Van Gogh captured on canvas in 1889. The north and west wings date from the sixteenth century, the south and east wings from the seventeenth, all being the work of Arles architect Jacques Peytret, designer of the city's town hall. The ground floor is connected to the outside by arcades bordering a walk which is duplicated on the first floor. The facades are stern, their small windows reflecting the hospital practice of the time.

Vincent Van Gogh at the Hôtel-Dieu

VAN GOGH was admitted to the Hôtel-Dieu in 1888, having mutilated his ear after an argument with Paul Gauguin, who had moved into the Maison Jaune, Van Gogh's home at the time. He was to be readmitted the following year for a nervous disorder, this time at the request of the residents of the Place Lamartine, who had sent a petition to the mayor. After treatment by Dr Félix Rey he left Arles and was interned at his own request in the asylum at Saint-Paul-de-Mausole, near Saint-Rémy-de-Provence.

LEAVING the asylum in a state of nervous exhaustion in May 1890, Van Gogh went to live in Auvers-sur-Oise, where he committed suicide two months later.

THE ARLES HÔTEL-DIEU continued to function until 1974, when the Joseph-Imbert hospital complex opened in the Fourchon district. When the last of its medical departments closed in 1986, the enormous building became a cultural centre. O.C.

Multimedia Library

THE MULTIMEDIA LIBRARY is the flagship of the municipal library service, which also includes four neighbourhood annexes –Barriol, Griffeuille, Trébon and Raphèle– and a mediabus.

REPLACING the municipal library –located in the old archbishop's palace– in 1989, the multimedia library

3

occupies the north wing of the Espace Van Gogh. It enjoys a remarkable architectural context in the form of the sixteenth and seventeenth century hospital buildings, a basically austere setting which, in the remarkable renovation by Denis Froidevaux and Jean-Louis Tetrel, has become luminously convivial and a pleasure to visit.

THIS CHANGE of location meant a total transformation for a library that already possessed a handsome collection of books and some 2,000 splendid old manuscripts. With the move it also acquired an art library, a record library –over 14,000 CDs– and a video selection of more than 6,000 films. This broadening of its range generated enormous enthusiasm and attracted a real diversity of new users.

MORE SIGNIFICANT change came with computerisation. Not only did this facilitate loans and user registration, it also provided the possibility of using the Internet for documentary research. Advances in this field have been so spectacular that users can now access France's national collective catalogue and its 14 million entries.

THUS THE multimedia library is constantly working to provide the broadest possible audience with maximum cultural possibilities. The quality and variety of its collections together with free provision of all services are eloquent testimony to this dedication.

J.-J.L.

Municipal archives

THE COLLECTION at the municipal archives is one of the most impressive in southern France in terms of quantity, antiquity, continuity and state of conservation.

THE ARCHIVES include parish and civil records, minutes of municipal council meetings, land registers and accounting documents –in most cases without a break from the Middle Ages down to the present.

AMONG THE MOST striking documents are two handsome registers recording the confirmation of privileges, the City statutes and the consulate charter. One of them, known as the "Black Book" because of the colour of its binding, dates from the late fourteenth century and contains two illuminated miniatures.

ALSO WORTHY of note are the ecclesiastical record known as the cartulary (c. 1210) and the fourteenth-century register containing the statutes of the Hospitallers of St John of Jerusalem (the Knights of Malta), sixty-three letters to the Arles consuls signed by Louis XIV and over five hundred maps of the city, its territory, its buildings
and its historic monuments from the sixteenth to the twentieth century.

FORMERLY stored in a large, specially equipped room in the town hall, the municipal archives were moved to the Espace Van Gogh in 1989.

S.R.

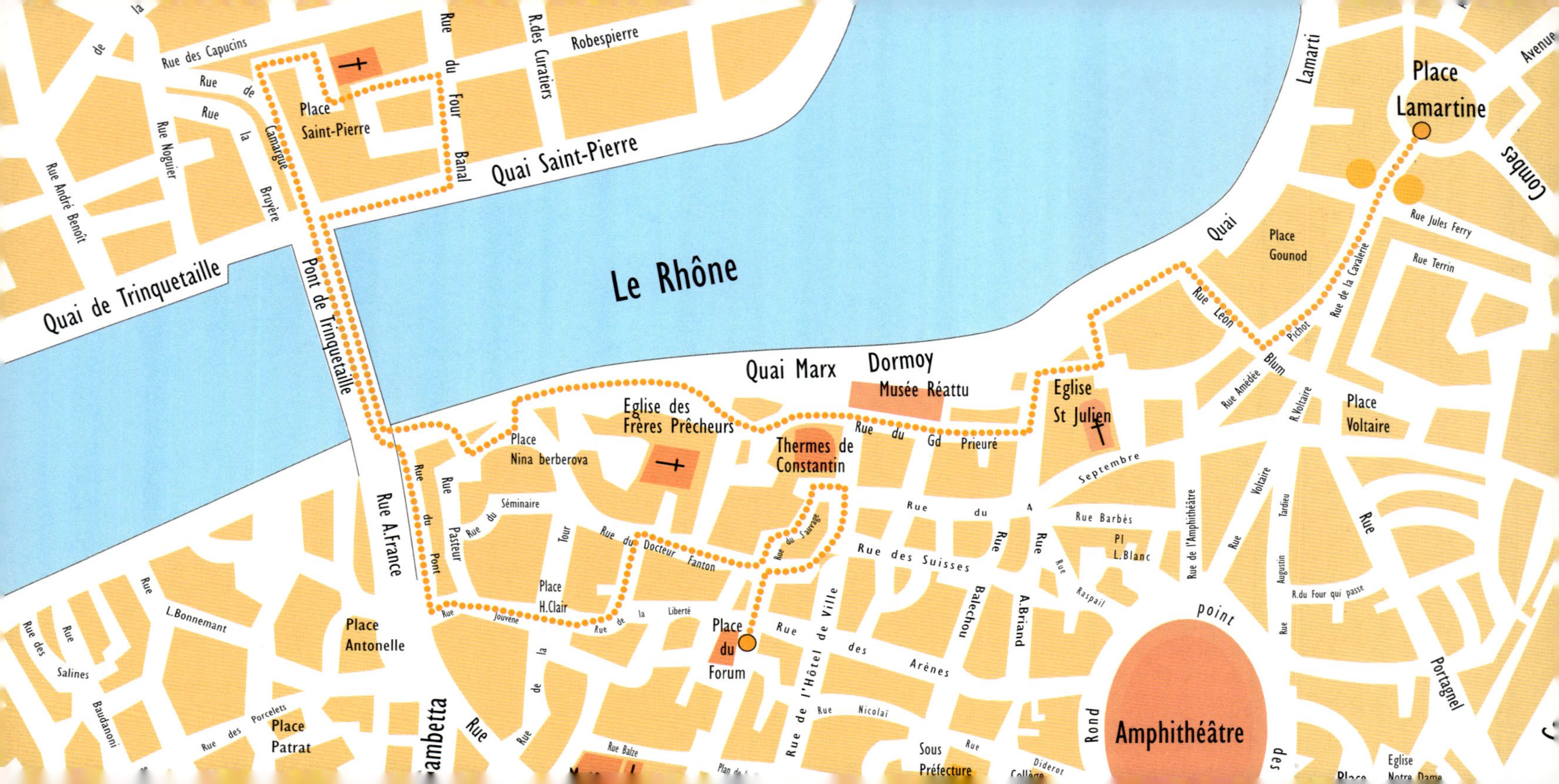
Le Rhône
Place Lamartine
Avenue
Combes
Lamarti
Rue Jules Ferry
Rue Terrin
Place Gounod
Quai
Rue de la Cavalerie
Pichot
Rue Léon Blum
Rue Amédée
R.Voltaire
Place Voltaire
Quai Marx Dormoy
Musée Réattu
Eglise St Julien
Rue du Gd Prieuré
Septembre
Rue Barbès
Pl L.Blanc
Rue de l'Amphithéâtre
Voltaire
Rue
Tardieu
Augustin
R.du Four qui passe
Rue
Portagnel
Rond point des
Amphithéâtre
Eglise Notre Dame
Rue du A
Rue A.Briand
Rue Raspail
Rue des Suisses
Rue Balechou
Rue des Arènes
Rue de l'Hôtel de Ville
Rue Nicolaï
Sous Préfecture
Rue Diderot
Collège
Thermes de Constantin
Rue du Sauvage
Place du Forum
Eglise des Frères Prêcheurs
Place Nina berberova
Rue du Séminaire
Rue Pasteur
Tour
Rue du Docteur Fanton
Place H.Clair
Rue Jouvène
Rue de la Liberté
Rue du Pont
Rue A.France
Rue de la
Rue Balze
Plan de la
Gambetta
Rue
Place Antonelle
Place Patrat
Rue des Porcelets
Rue L.Bonnemant
Rue des Salines
Baudanoni
Pont de Trinquetaille
Quai de Trinquetaille
Quai Saint-Pierre
Place Saint-Pierre
Rue du Four Banal
R.des Curatiers
Robespierre
Rue des Capucins
Rue de Camargue
Rue la Bruyère
Rue Noguier
Rue André Benoît
de la

From the Place Lamartine to the Place du Forum

The Rhône tour

The river is a key part of Arles' identity. This walk along the banks of the Rhône is one of the best ways of getting to understand the town described by the Roman poet Ausonius as the "twofold" Arles, which has stood on both sides of the water ever since antiquity; Arles and its protective banks; Arles, prestigious home of the Grand Priory of the Knights of Malta. After this riverside amble, we go onto the maze of small streets lined with churches and town-houses leading to the Place du Forum. Here we can soak up the town's atmosphere, its light and shade and busy café terraces.

1

2

1. Sculpted lion from the old railway bridge.
2. Amédée-Pichot fountain.

Beyond the walls, where once lay fields and pasture lands, the Place Lamartine marks the northern boundary of Arles' historic kernel. The square was laid out only in the nineteenth century, when the railway station was built. This was in 1871, when a garden was also planted here. This is where Van Gogh rented the famous "Yellow House" shown in his paintings. Destroyed by bombs in 1944, it stood in front of today's *Hôtel Terminus* et *Van Gogh*. We cross the Place Lamartine and enter the old town through the Porte de la Cavalerie.

Porte de la Cavalerie

La Cavalerie Quarter

THE PORTE de la Cavalerie is flanked by two round towers with bossages. It was rebuilt in the sixteenth century, when it had a drawbridge spanning the *roubine du roy*, a canal built to drain the marshland. This "royal" canal ran alongside the wall and into the Rhône. In the eighteenth century "half-moon" defences were added to the gate. This was subsequently demolished. In 1901, the drainage canal was covered over. O.C.

Taking the Rue de la Cavalerie, which is lined with buildings designed by the architects Vago and Van Migom after the bombing raids of 1944, we come to the Amédée-Pichot fountain.

Amédée-Pichot fountain

Corner of the Rue Amédée-Pichot and the Rue de la Cavalerie

THIS FOUNTAIN was built between 1884 and 1887 by Pierre-Amédée Pichot in memory of his father, the writer and journalist Amédée Pichot, born in Arles in 1796. To this end Pierre-Amédée bought up the house on the corner and had most of it demolished to make space for the fountain, facing

Commanderie de Sainte-Luce.

the Porte de la Cavalerie. The work was entrusted to the Parisian architect Joseph Flandrin. In the central medallion the Allegory of Poetry, based on the Raphael painting, was executed by local painter Paul Balze (1815-1884). The lion depicted in profile in the upper part is by Auguste Cain (1822-1894), a student of Rude and one of the finest animal sculptors of the nineteenth century. O.C.

Taking the Rue Amédée-Pichot then right into the Rue Léon-Blum, we come to the banks of Rhône, which were built up in around 1870 to protect Arles from flooding. Continuing behind the chevet of the Église Saint-Julien, we come to the Rue de Grille.

Hôtel de Biord

4, Rue de Grille

IN 1741, the Biords, a wealthy family of jurists, had the their family home extensively rebuilt to discreet and elegant effect. The three-storey facade features numerous windows in the style characteristic of the eighteenth-century, with a rectangular frame surmounted by a small arch. This mansion stood close to the walls built alongside the Rhône and near one of the city gates, the Porte de Rousset. It was also close to a number of religious buildings: the Grand Priory of the Order of Malta (now the Musée Réattu), the Église Saint-Julien and the Grands-Augustins building, which was demolished to make way for the Léon-Blum school in the 1950s. O.C.

We now turn right into the Rue du Grand-Prieuré, where, a few dozen metres down the road, we come to the Musée Réattu. Opposite this museum stands the Commanderie de Sainte-Luce.

Commanderie de Sainte-Luce

Rue du Grand-Prieuré

THIS BUILDING originally belonged to the Knights Templar. It then became the property of the Hospitallers of St John of Jerusalem (the Order of Malta). It comprises four parts. One is probably from the thirteenth century, two date to the fifteenth and the other was altered in the sixteenth century. The portal still has its Flamboyant Gothic decoration from the late fifteenth century. The edifice is articulated around a courtyard. Onto this gives a fine facade with richly decorated mullion windows and another, later facade (dated to 1587) with pilasters. Also remarkable is the hexagonal staircase tower in the corner pierced with small windows. Two handsome arcaded loggias also give onto the courtyard. One of these was built in the fifteenth century, the other in the sixteenth. The second is similar to the loggia in the outer courtyard of the Grand Priory, currently the Musée Réattu. O.C.

At the end of the Rue du Grand-Prieuré is the Rue Dominique-Maïsto, where we find the Baths of Constantine.

Musée Réattu

Formerly Grand Priory of the Knights of Malta

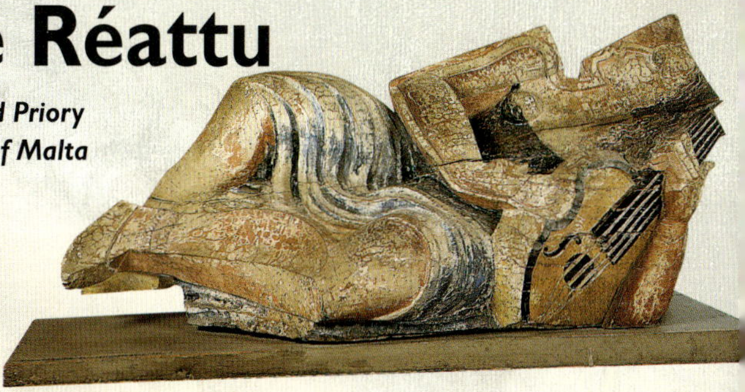

10, Rue du Grand-Prieuré
Tel. 04.90.49.38.34
Fax 04.90.49.36.97
E-mail musée.reattu.arles@provnet.fr

Openings:
1 - 31 Dec., and 2 - 31 Jan.
10.00-12.00, 14.00-16.30
1 - 28 Feb.
10.00-12.00, 14.00-17.00
1 - 31 March and 1 - 31 Oct.
10.00-12.30, 14.00-17.30
1 April - 30 Sept.
10.00-12.30, 14.00-19.00
2 - 30 Nov.
10.00-12.00, 14.00-17.00

The Musée Réattu, a fine arts museum, occupies two adjoining buildings on the banks of the Rhône that formerly belonged to the Order of Malta.

To the east stands the Commanderie de Saliers, built in the fifteenth century. This was the Arles residence of the Commander and knights, who were more usually to be found in the Camargue. They occupied the apartments around the courtyard, the southern facade of which is a fine example of seventeenth-century architecture. A room on the northern ground floor with superb vaulting was used to store grain from the Commandery's properties.

Overlookinng the river, the large first floor room was used as a studio by the painter Jacques Réattu. It still has its tapestries from a cycle on the *Seven Wonders of the World* said to have belonged to Queen Christina of Sweden. They are all that remains of the Grand Priory's pre-Revolutionary decoration.

To the west the old Commandery of

Above: L'Odalisque by Ossip Zadkine, 1932.

The old Grand Priory of the Knights of Malta.

Saint-Thomas de Trinquetaille was built in 1358, after the destruction of an earlier building, a house founded in the twelfth century at Trinquetaille by deserters from the Battle of Poitiers. IN 1562, after conflict between Catholics and Protestants at Saint-Gilles, and the sacking of the Grand Priory of the Tongue of Provence, the prior took refuge in Arles, in the Commandery of Saint-Thomas. In 1615, a decree by the Order confirmed it as the home of the Grand Commander. The Commandery was henceforth a Grand Priory, and as such the centre of a network of 48 commanderies located between Toulouse, home of the other Great Priory of the Tongue of Provence, and Geneva. Until the Revolution this was where the commanders held their assemblies, at least twice a year. Like the Commanderie de Saliers, the building is organised around a courtyard. Its size was reduced in 1640 when Honoré de Quiqueran-Beaujeu ordered the construction of a large ceremonial staircase to replace the old spiral staircase. Quiqueran also pierced the gallery overlooking the chapel at the southern end. The latter was built after 1503 by the commander of Trinquetaille, Melchior Cossa. It has a flat chevet and three bays with ribbed vaults. The keystones have emblazoned pendentives. The northern part of the building still has elements of the mullioned and latticed windows that were replaced by bigger windows in the eighteenth century. At the top of the building we can see some of the medieval crenellations and false machicoulis with superb gargoyles. Meetings were held on the first floor and the offices were on the upper floors. Archives were kept in the room over the chapel.

Jacques Réattu, a painter from Arles (1760-1833)

IN 1792, during the Revolution, the two buildings were confiscated in the name of the nation and sold off. Jacques Réattu bought the Commanderie de Saliers in 1796, adding the Grand Priory bit by bit between 1801 and 1827 (it had been divided up into 26 lots). Inspired by the riverside scenery, his aim was to create an artists' studio here –a forebear of the "Atelier du midi" that Van Gogh would dream of sixty years later.

AT RÉATTU'S DEATH in 1833 the buildings were inherited by his daughter, Élisabeth Grange, along with his works and private collection. Having no heirs herself, she sold the ensemble to the city of Arles in exchange for a life annuity, stipulating that there be a public museum of paintings to showcase her father's works. This opened in 1868.

Study of heads for St Paul, *by Jacques Réattu, 1827-1829.*

BORN IN ARLES in 1760, Réattu was the love child of Guillaume de Barrème de Chateaufort, a *gentilhomme* from Montpellier, and Catherine Raspal, sister of the painter Antoine Raspal, who no doubt taught his nephew the rudiments of his art. The young Réattu went up to Paris and studied in the ateliers of Julien and Regnault. In 1790 he won the prestigious Grand Prix de Rome with *Daniel Arresting the Elders.* In Rome he worked hard copying antiquities, drawing landscapes and producing the paintings that laureates were expected to present at regular intervals. The young man also espoused the ideals of the Revolution, expressing these in paintings such as

Prometheus Stealing the Sacred Fire (1792). However, anti-Revolutionary reaction forced him to flee Rome. He travelled from Naples to Marseille, where he began working on large-scale compositions in praise of the Revolution such as *The Triumph of Civilisation,* 1793 and *The Triumph of Liberty* (1794). Most importantly, he was commissioned to decorate the Église des Prêcheurs in Marseille for its transformation into a Temple of Reason (1794-1795). For this he proposed ten grisailles. Of the eight that were completed, six can be seen in the museum.

AFTER HIS MARRIAGE in 1798, Réattu let his activities as a painter lapse, only returning to the easel in 1818 for a series on Ovid's *Metamorphoses.* Above all, threw himself into a number of major decorative projects, such as the ceiling of the Grand Théâtre in Marseille (*Apollo and the Muses Casting Flowers at Time,* 1828) or propositions for the theatre at Nîmes (1821) and the town hall at Marseille (1826). In 1827-1829 he painted three canvases depicting the *Story of St Paul* for the church of Saint-Paul de Beaucaire. The splendid study of heads is one of his finest works.

The Sewing Workshop at Arles, *by Antoine Raspail, c. 1785.*

The first collections

THE HEART of the museum's historic collection comprises works by Réattu (including several hundred drawings) and from his own collection (paintings from the French and Italian schools, plus prints and drawings). Worthy of note here are Simon Vouet's superb *Self-portrait* (c. 1618), acquired by Réattu in Rome, a number of works by Antoine Raspal such as *L'Atelier de couture à Arles* (*The Sewing Workshop at Arles,* c. 1785) and *La Famille du peintre* (*The Painter's Family*, c. 1770-1780). To these can be added a number of Dutch paintings on permanent loan from the State (Houckgeest, Koedijk).

BEGINNING in the 1950s, the buildings were completely restored and the exhibitions and acquisitions policies were reoriented in favour of modern art. A number of key works entered the collections during these years, including a still life by Manguin, drawings and paintings by Henri Rousseau, two pieces by Zadkine: *Torse féminin* (*Female Torso*, 1935) and *L'Odalisque* (1932, a masterpiece of Cubist sculpture), plus *Le Griffu* (*The Clawed One*) by Germaine Richier (1952). These were the first works directly inspired by the magic of the setting.

Photography at the Musée Réattu

IN 1965 Lucien Clergue masterminded the creation of a photography section, the first in a French museum. Some four thousand works have since entered the collections.

IN ADDITION to early donations by photographers such as Richard Avedon, Cecil Beaton, Man Ray, Peter Beard, Werner Bischof, Izis, William Klein, Jean Dieuzaide, etc., or by collectors such as Jérôme Hill and Hélène Cingria, who contributed works by Ansel Adams, Berenice Abbott, Man Ray, Germaine Krull, Dora Maar and Edward Weston, there have been offerings from the many photographers taking part in the town's photography festival, the Rencontres Internationales de la Photographie (since 1970), including Ansel Adams, Judy Dater, Yousuf Karsh, André Kertész, Marc Riboud, Willy Ronis, Georges Tourdjman, Arthur Tress and Jerry Uelsmann.

The museum has since adopted a more directive, twofold approach, concentrating on "art photography" (Pascal Kern, Ton Zwerver, Jan Svenungsson and Alain Fleischer) on one side and, above all, illustrating the theme of "magical and mythical Arles." Commissions from Mimmo Jodice, Vasco Ascolini, Jacqueline Salmon and Yannick Hedel, plus acquisitions from other artists, have considerably enriched the collection and transformed the traditional image of the town.

Nude *by Edward Weston, 1936.*

The collection is presented in thematic and monographic exhibitions on the ground floor of the Grand Priory.

Painting and sculpture

THE YEAR 1971 was a particularly auspicious one for the museum's painting collection. This was when Picasso, who came regularly for the bullfights held in the amphitheatre, donated a marvellous and precious series of 57 dated and numbered drawings on his favourite themes: Pierrots, Harlequins, Musketeers and The Painter and His Model.

IN 1985, Jacqueline Picasso added the *Portrait of Maria Picasso Lopez* (1923), thus bringing mother and son together in a single homage. In 1990 the State reinforced this ensemble with the loan of Picasso's *Portrait de Lee Miller en Arlésienne* (*Lee Miller Dressed as an Arlesian*, 1937), a subtle homage to Vincent Van Gogh's *Portrait of Madame Ginoux*.

THE COLLECTION has also been strengthened by a number of acquisitions and donations. These include works by Bezombes, Mario Prassinos, Marchand, César, Arman, Buraglio, Bernard Pagès, Clauzel, Robelin, Ackling, Degottex, Morellet, Duport and Pol Bury.

MOST NOTABLY, there are two pieces by Pierre Alechinsky, which were

Pierrot and Harlequin *by Pablo Picasso, 1971.*

made either in Arles (*Soleil tournant [Spinning Sun]*, 1987) or nearby (*Érosion éolienne [Wind Erosion]*, 1988), and *Al Alimon* (1980) an extraordinary series by Mexican painter Alberto Gironella, done with two brushes, which was donated in 1996.

IN 1981, the museum began to commission sculptural works made on-site and inspired by the superb volumes of the cloister at Saint-Trophime or other local monuments. Among the artists invited to work in the city are Toni Grand (1981), Bernard Dejonghe (1986), Hélène Agofroy (1989) and Bernard Pagès. The result is a unique collection that draws on both sculpture and architecture in its homage to the *genius loci*; a collection that brings Arles' heritage alive as part of a constantly evolving present.

A.C. - M.M.

Thermes de Constantin

Rue Dominique-Maïsto

The hot room (caldarium) and the warm room (tepidarium) are open to visitors. The rest of the Baths of Constantine have been incorporated into neighbouring houses.

Open:

2 Nov. - 28 Feb.: 10.00-12.00, 14.00-17.00

1 March - 30 April: 9;00-12.00, 14.00-18.00

2 May - 30 Sept.: 9.00-19.00

1 Oct. - 31 Oct.: 9.00-12.00, 14.00-18.00

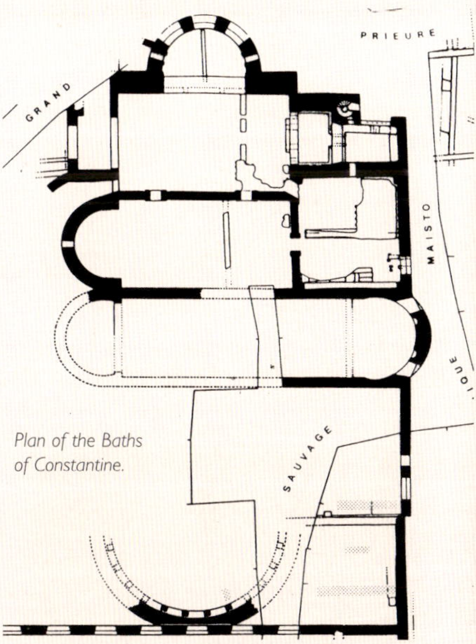

Plan of the Baths of Constantine.

Like any other Roman town, the colony of Arles had several thermal establishments. What we know about them varies considerably from one to another, but the three baths were known to have existed were all west of the *cardo*, the main north-south artery corresponding to today's Rue de l'Hôtel-de-Ville.

PROCEEDING from the south, we come first to the baths on the site of the Esplanade des Lices, built in the second century to the south of the Augustan fortifications. This complex is relatively well known, although its vestiges can no longer be seen. Much less is known about the baths located on the Place de la République, which were rediscovered in the seventeenth century during the erection of the obelisk. Other elements were discovered during the construction of the Chamber of Commerce, now the Caisse d'Épargne, on the west side of the square.

A massive building of stone and brick

BUT the best known and the best preserved are the northern baths; known as the Thermes de Cosntantin, or Thermes de la Trouille. These go from the Place du Sauvage to the banks of the Rhône. It was long thought that this massive stone and brick building, vestiges of which could be found throughout houses in this quarter, was the palace that Emperor Constantine built at the beginning of the fourth century. We know that there was a palace belonging to the Counts of Provence in this quarter in the thirteenth and fourteenth centuries, the Palais de Trullia. However, excavation of the ruins in the late nineteenth century showed that the building was in fact a bathhouse.

TODAY, only the northern part of the baths is

accessible, representing essentially the hot rooms and the ancillary rooms.

Disposition of the Baths

ALTHOUGH there is virtually nothing left of the Roman *suspensura* (the floor suspended over the hypocaust), it is fairly easy to imagine how this part of the baths was laid out. The main element here is the *caldarium*, the hot room, with its vaulted bath. The central room was flanked by two other rectangular baths. We can still see the marble floor and some of the *tubuli*, the hollow bricks used to heat the walls and reduce condensation, belonging to the one on the eastern side. The real heating room was on the northeastern corner of the building. It served another room to the south and the eastern bath of the *caldarium*, which was directly heated by a fire in its southwest corner.

THE CALDARIUM had two doors opening onto the *tepidarium*, or warm room, to the south. We can still see its western apse. Recently excavated, this feature has been filled pending restoration work. Its wall was hollowed out to accommodate a fire.

TO THE EAST of this room we find the remains of another heated room. Almost a perfect square, it can also be reached from the *caldarium* through an oblique door. It must have been particularly well heated, what with the heating room and the fire in the east wall. It was most probably the *laconicum*, another very hot room.

THE REST of the complex has yet to be excavated. However, such as they are, these often remarkably well preserved vestiges do allow us to establish its general form. For example, the houses abutting the *tepidarium* to the south incorporate large sections of wall belonging to the *frigidarium* (cold bath). This was a large rectangular room with an apse at each end. The form of the eastern one can still be made out. Parts of the eastern wall have been found beyond the Place du Sauvage, but we do not know how far the southern side extended, let alone the extent of the west side.

Vestiges and interior of the Baths of Constantine.

A likely chronology: from the late third to the early fourth century

THIS CONSTRUCTION, in which beds of rag-stone alternate with levelling courses of brick is traditionally dated to the age of Constantine, who is credited with the city's renaissance after the upheavals of the third century. Recent excavation work, particularly in the western apse of the *tepidarium*, has provided some confirmation of this view by dating the work to a period between the late third century and the early fourth. It also looks, quite logically, as if there were several phases of restoration and maintenance work.

AT SEVERAL points traces of earlier constructions have been found among the ruins. At the northwestern corner of the *caldarium*, for example, it is still possible to see an accumulation of blocks of stone which may well be the remains of a tower from the proto-historical walls that protected the town on the river side. Also, at the bottom of the southern wall in the *laconicum* we can still see the levelling masonry work for a course of stones which has been incorporated into the floor. Of course, it is difficult to interpret these vestiges with any certainty, but it is possible that there was an earlier bath house.

Extension of the baths up to the fifth century

THE BATHS were limited at the southern end by a building running from east to west which, although it has sometimes been thought part of the whole, was in fact independent. This is a vast rectangular hall measuring 57 by 21 metres. It was lit by the large windows in its lateral walls. The construction, which is remarkably well preserved, contained as it is within the walls of a hotel, the *Hôtel d'Arlatan*, had its main entrance on the west side and may have ended at the east with an apse. A column from its facade can still be seen in one of the hotel reception rooms. Although the excavation work could not provide a precise date for this basilical hall, it must be later than the Baths of Constantine. It could well have been an audience and reception hall, and may have been built when the Prefect of the Gauls established his court in Arles in the late fourth or early fifth century.

FINALLY, during the fifth century a large apse, no doubt covering a cold pool, was built against the north wall of the basilica, almost opposite the apse of the caldarium in the Baths of Constantine. This was the last extension to the Baths before they were left derelict. Excavation work around this apse, and around that of the *tepidarium*, has revealed that by the early sixth century the Baths were filled with earth. M.H.

Hôtel de L'Hoste.

Continuing along the Rue du Grand-Prieuré, we come to the Hôtel de L'Hoste on the right.

Hôtel de L'Hoste

16, Rue du Grand-Prieuré

BUILT at the end of the seventeenth century, this townhouse belonged to the L'Hostes, a family of reputable doctors. The style of the three-storey facade is in fact closer to that of early seventeenth-century townhouses than to the neo-classical rigour characteristic of its period. We may note the framing of the door with its Corinthian columns and frieze of rinceaus. Also worthy of admiration are the highly refined panels of the second storey with their sculpted decoration of leaves and foliage. O.C.

Turning down the street facing the Hôtel de L'Hoste, we come to the Hôtel de Truchet, which belonged to Michel de Truchet (1766-1841), a poet and passionate scholar of Provençal culture. It has a fine, very simple classical facade which is of particular interest for the harmonious disposition of its windows. Coming back into the Rue du Grand-Prieuré, we now head towards the Église des Dominicains, also known as the Preaching Friars.

Église des Dominicains

Quai Marx-Dormoy

THE ORDER of the Preaching Friars, founded in around 1215 by St Dominic, established a monastery outside the city walls in 1231. When this was destroyed

1

2

1. Église des Dominicains: Portal.
2. Église Saint-Martin.
3. The "Lion Bridge," destroyed during the Second World War.
4. The right bank of the Rhône seen from Trinquetaille.

in 1361, the Dominicans sought refuge behind the ramparts. Their new house was in the centre of the Juiverie ("Jews' quarter"), to the west of the present church. These new premises soon became cramped and the Dominicans decided to build a new church. Construction work lasted from 1448 to 1499, when the edifice was consecrated under the name of Notre-Dame-de-Confort.
BUILT in the Southern Gothic style, the church has a single nave with five bays leading to lower-ceilinged side chapels. The fairly shallow polygonal apse is also lower than the nave. The vault of the nave has intersecting ribs. The thrust of the nave, with its intersecting rib vault, is contained by external abutments linked by flying buttresses, with light from windows placed between the abutments. The facade is divided into two parts by a hexagonal stairway turret affording access to the organ loft and to the roof, from which there rises the wall belfry. There were two doors, one, to the north of the turret, for the faithful, and the other, to the south, for the monks. There was a third entrance to the southeast, in the fourth bay. The church underwent several phases of rebuilding and enlargement. The cloister, for example, was added between 1560 and 1581.
A Flamboyant Gothic door gave worshippers access to the church. In the early seventeenth century the southern entrance was embellished by an antechapel with rib vaulting. In those days, the building was considered one of the city's finest churches for the decoration of the nave and chapels. After the Revolution the church and convent buildings were sold off as state property. At the end of the nineteenth century the cloister was partially destroyed to allow construction of a waterworks in the Rue du Docteur-Fanton. In 1921 the church became a listed historical monument and six decades later, in 1981, it was bought up by the municipality. The constructions that had later been grafted onto the church were demolished and, after a series of archaeological digs between 1985 and 1988, it is now being restored.
THE WORK so far has revealed that the northern pillars of the nave are supported on an ancient wall in perfectly dressed stone with bossages on either side, directly below. The same would seem to be true of the pillars on the southern side. These two ancient walls were still clearly visible in the fifteenth century, and were what determined the width of the nave. M.H.

Following the Rhône along the Quai Marx-Dormoy, we reach a section of the old walls that formeded part of the medieval riverside ramparts protecting the city from enemy attacks and flooding. On the left is the Église Saint-Martin.

Église Saint-Martin

Quai Marx-Dormoy

LOCATED in the Méjan quarter, Saint-Martin goes back to the ninth century. In the fifteenth century its bell-tower was totally rebuilt and, in the following century, the church was deemed too small and, with the exception of the polygonal apse which became a chapel, was demolished before being rebuilt with a new orientation. The new building adopted a late Gothic style, but with a Louis XIII-style facade. Saint-Martin was open to the parish community and also served as a chapel for a nearby seminary.

3

4

Because of its position near the Rhône this place of worship was also used as a sanctuary for the bodies of the drowned, whose tombs were kept here. Inside we can still see an inscription signalling the tombs of plague victims. In fact, these remained intact when the building was deconsecrated and sold off as national property during the Revolution. In 1982 the church was converted into a concert hall. M.B.

We now take the Trinquetaille bridge across the Rhône. From the other side of the river there is a fine view of Arles.

Trinquetaille quarter

TODAY'S Trinquetaille quarter was of considerable importance during the Roman period as the location of the warehouses serving the port. In the second century, urban growth led to development of the area with the construction of sumptuous villas (their mosaics can be seen in the Musée de l'Arles Antique).

IT WAS HERE, too, that a glassworks was built in the eighteenth century. Its successor is still here today (nearer the Rue de la Verrerie). It is the only industrial establishment in Arles to date from the Ancien Régime. O.C.

The Rhône: port, banks and bridges

EVER SINCE men have lived on the site now occupied by Arles, the river has played a decisive role as an artery, making Arles a key point for traffic linking the European continent to the Mediterranean Sea. In the period of Greek domination, a toll and control station was built on the hill overlooking the Rhône. This stimulated the development of what was one of the great trading counters of the Ancient World. Later, the Roman presence consolidated Arles' role as a hub for trade between Italy, Spain and North Africa. The commercial port was most probably located in today's Trinquetaille quarter, which is where goods carried by sea were transferred to river vessels. Traces of these exchanges have been found on the river bed and out to sea. The diversity and quantity of material and, in particular, the great variety of amphoras discovered here, convey the vitality of trade in this period.

IN MEDIEVAL TIMES, and also in more recent centuries, levels of activity in the port diminished somewhat as a result of the movements of the Rhône but also because of endemic piracy. While it retained a working connection to the Mediterranean, and in spite of upturns (most notably in the seventeenth century), the port never recovered the importance it had in Antiquity. In the nineteenth century, the advent of steamships and, above all, construction of the Paris-Lyon-Méditerranée railway line, further undermined the role of Arles with its old-fashioned *tartanes* and lighters.

IN 1913 Arles lost its maritime status and the town was demoted from a port to a simple point of transit. However, the construction of a new trading port a little further upstream of the town gave the town's fluvio-maritime activity a new lease of life.

1. Églis Saint-Pierre de Trinquetaille: Stained glass by Alfred Manessier.

2. Hôtel Lestang-Parade.
3. Hôtel Léautaud de Donines.

River banks and bridges

BEFORE the nineteenth century, the town's river activities were all centred on the fairly simple quays along the Rhône. These were used for loading and unloading boats, but also served –not always that effectively– to protect the town from flooding. After a series of floods in the middle of the twentieth century, an ambitious building programme was implemented, giving the riverside its present appearance. However, maintenance was fairly slack until the floods of 1993-1994, and vital restoration work is now being carried out.

AS A TRADING city built along a major river, Arles also needed serviceable bridges. The boat bridges that spanned the river in ancient and medieval times were often carried away by the rising waters. Later, they were temporarily replaced by a trail ferry guided by a steel cable running from one bank to another. In 1865 a railway bridge was built on the Arles-Lunel line used to bring coal from La Grand'Combe (Gard department). It was destroyed during the Second World War but its piers are still visible, as are the two entrances decorated with lions by the local sculptor Dieudonné (1827-1897), which led to the structure being known as the "Lion Bridge". In 1875 a road bridge finally connected Arles and the outlying Trinquetaille quarter. It replaced the old boat bridge. This road bridge was also destroyed in 1944 but was rebuilt after the war. In 1970, an expressway link to Nîmes was added. P.R.

If we take the passage under the buildings on the Quai Saint-Pierre, we will come to the Place Saint-Pierre and the church of the same name.

Église Saint-Pierre de Trinquetaille

Place Saint-Pierre

THE PARISH of Saint-Pierre, on the right bank of the Rhône, is one of the oldest parts of Arles. Its religious buildings have been repeatedly ruined by floods. After the Revolution, an old Capuchin chapel became its new parish church. When this too was destroyed during the bombing raids of 1944, a new one was commissioned from Pierre Vago, a student of Auguste Perret who also designed the church of Saint-Pie X at Lourdes. Work began in 1952. The extremely pared-down style of architecture deployed by Vago at Saint-Pierre has proved coherent with the kind of urban development chosen for Arles during the period of postwar reconstruction.

INSIDE the church, a late eighteenth-century marble sculpture of the Virgin Mary, redolent in style of the Genoese sculptor Filippo Parodi, is all that is left of the furniture from the earlier church. The decor of this new building (altars, ambos, confessionals) was commissioned from the sculptor Navarre, who also made the large terracotta Christ raised up above the altar. The Way of the Cross is by a local artist, Miguel Deveze, and the stained glass in the baptistery is by Jean-Luc Perrot. As for the two large stained glass windows, measuring 12 square metres, they were commissioned from Alfred Manessier. This painter also donated the 22 small stained glass windows to the town of Arles in 1973. M.B.

We now come back over the Rhône in order to head into the town centre via the Rue du Pont.

3

Hôtel Lestang-Parade

15, Rue du Pont

The Lestang-Parades were an illustrious Provençal family. A number of its members were councillors at the parliament in Aix. The family rebuilt this townhouse in 1740. The edifice is remarkable for the stylisation of the facade with its majestic porch, the vertical rhythm of its large, smooth Corinthian pilasters with projections and its broad pediment with brackets. Now somewhat spoilt by shops at the bottom, the design is redolent of the classical architecture built in Paris by Gabriel during the same period. O.C.

A little further on, to the left, we take the Rue Jouvène, which leads us to the Place Honoré-Clair (named after the local historian and archaeologist who worked on the clearance of the amphitheatre and Roman theatre). On the left stands the Hôtel Léautaud de Donines.

Hôtel Léautaud de Donines

Banque de France

Rue de la Liberté

For many years this three-storey townhouse was the property of the Grille family. In the nineteenth century it was bought up by the Count Léautaud de Donines. Although much altered, it retains the old eighteenth-century architraves and, in the upper parts, elements of the original fifteenth century fortified architecture. In the twentieth century the Hôtel Léautaud de Donines was attributed to the Banque de France. O.C.

Continuing along the Rue de la Liberté, we pass the fine porch of the Hôtel de la Tour du Brau (sixteenth century) and reach the Rue des Pénitents-Bleus. Here we can see the southern side of the Dominican church against which the chapel of the Blue Penitents once stood., We now enter the Rue du Docteur-Fanton, formerly the Rue Neuve, the old centre of what, in the Middle Ages, was a sizeable Jewish quarter ("La Juiverie"). The synagogue was destroyed in 1484 during a riot, as were a number of other buildings belonging to Jews. Arles' Jewish community was banished from the city in 1498.

Old waterworks

34, Rue du Docteur-Fanton

This building, which now houses a number of municipal services, was built between 1863 and 1867 by Auguste Véran. With its rigid and severe appearance, this building is typical of the municipal and industrial architecture of the late nineteenth century. Its central section takes the form of a large hall divided up into two levels.

The lower part is wholly taken up by a monumental door offering access to a large vestibule. The upper part displays a neoclassical architectural vocabulary. The edifice is flanked by smaller buildings which are plain and functional. When it was decided that a waterworks should be built in order to provide the townspeople with running water, the municipality was obliged to raise a loan of 220,000 francs. O.C.

We now retrace our steps as far as the Rue du Sauvage, on the left. This was

1

2

once the northern end of the old Forum. Roman vestiges were incorporated into the old Arlatan de Beaumont townhouse, which is now a hotel.

Hôtel Arlatan de Beaumont

Hôtel d'Arlatan

26, Rue du Sauvage

THE D'ARLATAN family is known to have lived in Arles since the twelfth century. In 1448, Jean d'Arlatan, administrator for King René, rid the Crau area of a wild beast that was ravaging the countryside, devastating the fields of kermes oaks where "vermilion of Provence" (safflower) was harvested. The hero's reward was a prerogative over the crop, to be inherited by his descendants. Behind the severe classical three-storey facade, which was rebuilt in the eighteenth century, we find some fine sixteenth-century apartments overlooking a restored courtyard which still has elements of its old spiral staircase, a loggia and windows dating from various periods of the construction (twelfth to eighteenth centuries). O.C.

The *Hôtel d'Arlatan* and its Roman remains

IN 1988, when work was being done on the cellars of the hotel a large moulded block was discovered. It was no doubt a pedestal that supported a statue or other monument that leant against the podium of a portico situated up on the opposite side (vestiges can be seen from the Rue du Sauvage and in the hotel). This monumental ensemble, which can be linked to other elements found in cellars nearby, can be dated to the years 30-20 AD. It is no doubt related to the construction of a large Roman basilica (fifth century), remains of which can also be seen in the hotel. It is part of the first urban realisations after foundation of the Roman colony. M.H.

Opposite the Hôtel Arlatan, note the Hôtel de Monblanc.

Hôtel de Monblanc

Rue du Sauvage

IN ADDITION to their Arles home, the Monblancs, part of the local nobility, also owned a château at Maussanne. Looking through the gate of the Hôtel de Montblanc we can appreciate the charm of its courtyard and its architectural qualities. The main feature is the four-floor corner tower (second half of the sixteenth century). Its small windows framed by columns or pilasters show the refinement attained here by neo-antique architecture during the Renaissance. O.C.

We now turn back and head toward the Place du Forum.

Place du Forum

THE HEART of modern Arles, the Place du Forum combines a very lively present with a rich history. There was a square here in Roman times, down from the

1. Hôtel Arlatan de Beaumont.
2. Hôtel de Monblanc.
3. Place du Forum.

3

great colonnade of the forum. In the Middle Ages the square was called the Place du Sétier (a sétier was a measure of wheat). It was the site of a market, hence its other name of Place des Herbes. This important site for trade and business even had its notaries' shops. In 1684, the city council decided to build a hall to accommodate the agricultural workers who hired out their labour at harvest time. This practice, which continued until the 1900s, explains the name Place aux Hommes, which can still be seen here and there. This market building, which is no longer here, was built by Antoine I Guibert in 1693. In the eighteenth century, to the west of the square, they built the Juridiction des Marchands, the period equivalent of a chamber of commerce. Today, the establishments around the Place du Forum include the famous *Café Van Gogh,* which the eponymous artist depicted in his famous 1888 painting, *Le Café, la nuit* (*Night Café*). In 1909 a statue of the poet Frédéric Mistral was placed on the square. Sculpted by Théodore Rivière, an artist from Toulouse, the monument includes a medallion of Mireille, the eponymous heroine of Mistral's most famous work, by Férigoule, a sculptor and director of the Musée d'Arles. It was inaugurated by Mistral himself, on the fiftieth anniversary of his writing *Mireille.* O.C.

The Columms on the Place du Forum

TOGETHER with the vestiges in the *Hôtel d'Arlatan* and a tower in the Rue de la Liberté, the two Corinthian columns on the Place du Forum surmounted by a fragment of pediment are part of an ensemble of elements that have survived because of their incorporation in medieval Arles. In 1366, two owners disputed the right to the columns and were awarded one each. Partially hidden by later constructions, as we can see from a mid-seventeenth-century print, the columns were restored in the eighteenth century. THESE COLUMNS, along with half of the pediment, belonged to a tetrastyle facade (with four columns at the front) ten metres wide. The columns themselves, including the base and capital, were 8.85 metres high. The facade, which was designed to open onto the current Place du Forum, was the result of extending a building running perpendicular to the northern portico of the Roman forum, which had been modified in Late Antiquity. This facade may have been built using bits of older constructions, which would explain why the columns and capitals do not match up. The capitals and pediment date from the late first or early second century.

THE MAJESTY of this facade, which rose over 15 metres above the square below, and which could be reached by a broad flight of stairs, was emphasised by the large inscription in bronze letters that used to adorn the architrave and the frieze. We can clearly see the holes where these were attached. In the late eighteenth century there was an attempt to reconstitute the first three lines of the inscription, based on a study of their position. They were thought to form a dedication to Constantine II (337-340) and his forebears. A more recent analysis of the whole inscription would indicate that the dedicatee was actually Constantine the Great. The writing would then date to between 324 and 326. M.H.

Le Rhône
Voie express
Quai de la Roquette
Tour de l'Ecorchoir
Pavillon du Canal
Chemin de Barriol
Musée de l'Arles antique
Avenue de la Ière
RN 113
Avenue Sixte Qu
Boulevard Georges Clemenceau
Boulevare
Place Antonelle
Place Patrat
Place Genive
Eglise St Césaire
Espace Van Gogh Médiathèque
Théâtre Municipal
Museon Arlaten
Mairie
Place de la République
Place du Forum
Place H.Clair
Temple Protestant
Bourse du Travail
ANPE
Rue Gambetta
Rue de la République
L.Bonnemant
Rue des Salines
Rue Baudanoni
Rue des Porcelets
Rue de la Roquette
Rue W.Rousseau
Rue de la Croix Rouge
Rue Genive
Rue Taquin
Rue Bibion
Rue Raillon
Rue Trianon
R.Courte
R. Corneille
R. Racine
Rue Th. Rives
Rue du Plan du Bourg
Rue Lagoy
R. Bellon
Rue de Chartrouse
R. des Mariniers
Rue Molière
R. Jean Granaud
Rue Molière
Rue de la Rotonde
Rue J.Jaurès
Rue Balze
Rue de la Liberté
Rue Jouvène
Pont
Fanton
Bd de Craponne
Rue des Frères
Raveaux
Rue Cornillon
Sadi Carnot
Rue Parmentier
Bessier
Fernand
Rue Etienne
Rue Couturier
Leclerc
Gauthier
Zola

From the Museon Arlaten to the Musée de l'Arles Antique

The Vieux-Bourg tour

1. Promenaders on the Alyscamps *by E. Tassy, 1797.*
2. Lavender Pickers at the Pont de l'Observance *by Antoine Raspail.*
3. *Model of the Roman circus.*

1

2

3

Starting outside the Trinitarian chapel and the Museon Arlaten, this circuit takes us along what is one of Arles' main thoroughfares, the Rue de la République. This street is lined with many fine buildings that were once occupied by members of the nobility and clergy. Nowadays it is the heart of central Arles' main shopping area. Going beyond the Rue Gambetta and continuing in the direction of the Rhône, we come to one of the town's most picturesque quarters: La Roquette. After exploring there we reach the quarter of the old Roman circus and the Musée de l'Arles Antique.

Chapelle des Trinitaires

38, Rue de la République

THE FACADE of this Trinitarian chapel was completely revamped by the architect Auguste Véran in 1884. Hence its eclectic style. Note the very prominent arch-stones on its large round-arched porch. In the centre of the facade we see an imposing Renaissance-style window with a curved pediment, mullions and cross-bars, while the whole building is surmounted by a wide dentellated pediment. On the left and right sides, the facade is framed by large quoins.
THE ORDER of Trinitarians, whose mission was to ransom captives taken into slavery by the Barbary States, was founded in 1198 by St John of Math and St Felix of Valois. It set up a house in Arles shortly afterwards, between the Vieux-Bourg and the Méjan, beside the hospital of the Holy Spirit, known then as Saint-Esprit du Bourg. In 1199, John of Math returned to Rome and, on his way through Arles, recruited four monks –Boniface, Osbert, Matthieu and Vital– who founded the Trinitarian house here. They were given a warm welcome by the people of Arles, although it was not until 1203 that the congregation was granted official recognition and was able to build its first church and cloister and establish a cemetery. However, this extensive tract of land owned by the Trinitarian brothers was cut back in 1253 when the city walls were rebuilt and extended, and then reduced a second time in 1573 for the construction of the imposing Hôtel-Dieu du Saint-Esprit, with its church and cemetery.
ALTHOUGH "extremely small and in ruins", the house managed to survive in its original state until 1604. In 1620 construction work began on a new church and a new monastery. The old buildings were razed, thereby clearing a spacious platform. The first stone of the new church was laid in 1630 and it was dedicated to the Trinity and St Roch. The Trinitarians had negotiated to buy the relics of this Montpellier-born saint

Chapelle des Trinitaires

who was thought to offer protection against the plague.

THE CHURCH was deconsecrated during the Revolution, confiscated and then sold off as national property. While the convent building was subsequently demolished, we can still see the nave of the church. Built in the late Gothic style, it has a pentagonal apse with, at its centre, a presentation of the arms of the Perrin family, whose townhouse stands nearby. The top of the church is encircled by a classical cornice with corbelling and the centre of its vault is embossed with the Trinitarian pattée cross (with widened extremities) in gules and azure, which also appears on the lateral pillars. An ogival chancel arch supporting the city's coat of arms separates the choir from the nave. The latter was originally lit by eight high windows, although four of these have now been walled in. The seventeenth-century facade featured a portal embellished with a pediment supported by two Corinthian columns.

SOME PARTS of the galleries in the cloister have been incorporated into the shop buildings to the right of the church, in the street. This cloister originally consisted of a series of round arches edged with a thick torus. The upper level roof was supported by a series of small columns with simple capitals. The chevet is perfectly visible from inside the Médiathèque. The Trinitarian complex was sold to the hospices of Arles in 1792. Until recently it was occupied by shops, but its future rehabilitation will make it a living addition to Arles' heritage. M.B.

Opposite the Trinitarian chapel stands the Museon Arlaten.

The leading ethnographic museum in the South of France, the Museon Arlaten first opened in 1899. Then, in 1906, it was installed in the old Jesuit college. It was now possible to properly showcase its collection of everyday objects worthy of being kept for posterity as records of the life and traditions of old Provence.

From the Hôtel Laval-Castellane to the Jesuit College

BETWEEN 1471 AND 1505, the Castellanes, the lords of Fos and Laval de Chanant, who were allied with the Porcelets family of Arles, built a spacious residence in the Hôtel-Dieu quarter, near the house of the Trinitarians. A hexagonal tower on the north wing contained a wide spiral staircase. Capped with merlons, gargoyles and corner watchtowers, the building opened onto an inner courtyard as well as onto the street via wide crossings with multiple ribs and moulded architraves –a decorative style characteristic of Provençal Renaissance architecture and particularly prominent in the buildings of Avignon.

THE HÔTEL was inherited by the Marquis of Calvisson. He sold it to the "Company of Jesus", for whom it replaced the smaller teaching premises they had been using on the site of the Roman theatre. In 1652 the Jesuits built a chapel to the north of this palatial residence then bought various strips of land close to the Hôtel de Broglio, along the Rue de la Trinité, in order to extend their establishment.

BETWEEN 1738 AND 1748, the city financed the rebuilding of the southern part of the school. The design was by Mauric, an architect from Nîmes, while Jacques Imbert, a colleague from Arles, supervised construction with the assistance of Jean-Baptiste Perre. This building capped by a triangular pediment is symmetrically organised on three levels

Museon Arlaten

Musée départemental d'ethnographie

1

2

1. Mme de Privat and Her Daughters by Antoine Raspail.
2. Commemorative bowl of the Club de la Chiffonne, 18th century.

29, Rue de la République

Tel. 04.90.93.58.11

Fax 04 90 93 80 55

Open:

October – March: 9.30-12.30 14.00-17.00

April, May: 9.30-12.30,

14.00-18.00

June – August: 9.30-13.00 14.00-18.30

September: 9.30 -12.30 14.00-18.00

Closed on Mondays (except in July, August and September) and bank holidays (1 January, 1 May, 1 Nov., 25 Dec.).

around a monumental door surmounted by a balcony. It links with the inner courtyard via a hall whose ceiling evinces remarkable mastery of stone cutting, and opens onto a series of galleries. However, the abolition of the Jesuits by the Parliament of Provence in 1763 forced the Company to leave the city, leaving the decoration unfinished. The building became a municipal school in the nineteenth century. In 1906 the municipality attributed it to the Provençal ethnographic museum created by Frédéric Mistral in 1899, recognising that it offered an ideal setting for a new presentation. At the same time the second-century archaeological remains found in the cellars beneath the courtyard were excavated. These consist of a semicircular wall punctuated by niches and columns defining a paved public space that linked with the crypto-porticus. This monument constituted one of the monumental entrances to the Roman Forum.

Frédéric Mistral and the Museon arlaten

BORN into a peasant family, the poet Frédéric Mistral (1830-1914) became a committed proponent of the linguistic and cultural renaissance of his region when he was a young man. In 1854 he

created the Félibrige with six friends. His poems in praise of Provence, glorifying its history and legends, won him a growing reputation which turned into fame with the publication of *Mireiò*. Acclaimed by Lamartine, Mistral promoted Provençal identity in his public talks. He also compiled a dictionary. In 1895 he began research on popular practices and customs in his native province, preserving his material so as to create one of France's first regional ethnography museums. These objects and documents recorded a way of life threatened by the upheavals of urban and rural life at the onset of the new century. Mistral assembled them to form what he defined as a "poem for people who can't read".

1

2

The Museon collections

DONATED by generations of Provençals, some thirty thousand objects ranging from the humble to the magnificent bear witness to ways of life and work and mentalities in the lower Rhône valley during the eighteenth and nineteenth centuries. This is an enthusiast's attempt to stop time and glorify the culture of a region. Mistral's plan for the presentation of these objects has been partially maintained on the first floor of the museum. It contributes to the exhibit's seductive, old-fashioned atmosphere while arousing visitors' curiosity.

THE DISPLAY begins with three rooms devoted to the traditional costumes of Basse-Provence. Pride of place is given to the spectacular women's costumes of the Arles area. NEXT, domestic life in the *mas* (traditional houses) and urban houses is evoked by an accumulation of furniture (wardrobes, chests of drawers, bolting reels, kneading troughs) whose decoration reflects a pronounced love of nature. This great tableau of the life of yesteryear also includes everyday objects such as oil lamps, wool winders and chafing dishes. FURTHER ON, the beliefs, superstitions and festivities of Provençal society are conjured up through an accumulation of objects such as wax monsters (the Tarasque in its Saint-Éloi feast day trappings), precious amulets, figurative pastries, holy images and reliquaries. THIS PRESENTATION culminates with two recreations featuring mannequins. One illustrates the key moment in the ages of man, as these were perceived in the nineteenth century, with symbolic gifts being offered to a young mother; the other captures the high point of the annual cycle with the ritual blessing over the Yule log on Christmas Eve. ON THE SECOND FLOOR, which was opened in 1940, we come to the section about the history of Arles and Provence up to the creation of the Félibrige. Other rooms present agricultural and crafts tools that tell us about life in the Crau, the Camargue or the Alpilles regions. A Camargue-style hut made from reeds and wood vividly conveys the distinctive character of that particular vernacular architecture.

D.S.-H.

3

1. Arlésienne with the Venus of Arles *by Augustin Dumas, 1860.*
2. Portrait of an Arlésienne *by Antoine Raspail, c. 1785.*
3. *Fan, late 18th century.*

1

2

3

4

5

1. Hôtel de la Lauzière.
2. Hôtel de Méjanes.
3. Hôtel Laurent de Beaujeu.
4. Hôtel Icard-Duquesne.
5. The old Hôtel-Dieu, Rue du Lau.

Going back up the Rue de la République on the left, we make our way to the Hôtel de la Lauzière.

Hôtel de la Lauzière

42, Rue de la République

PROBABLY built in the early seventeenth century by the Chartroux family which, although of modest origins, had produced one or two brave soldiers, this townhouse was later bought by an aristocrat, Marie de Noble de la Lauzière, in 1727, who came from an intellectually and militarily distinguished family. The De la Lauzières subsequently had the facade of the townhouse rebuilt, probably in the late eighteenth century. The very restrained decoration chosen at this time contrasts with the extravagance of the original door, which has fortunately been preserved. Indeed, this is one of the finest doors in Arles. Characteristic of the Mannerist style popular in the years 1610-1620, its rich decoration features some quite remarkable twisted columns set on plinths with Corinthian capitals supporting an entablature and frieze decorated with rinceaus and a triangular pediment with bracketing, flanked on the right and the left with a decoration of volutes. O.C.

Opposite the former Hôtel de la Lauzière stands the former Hôtel de Méjanes, now occupied by the Société Générale bank. It was built in the seventeenth century by the Marquis of Méjanes, a learned collector who bequeathed his superb library to the city of Aix-en-Provence. Making our way back we go down the Rue de la République to the Rue Du Lau on the left, named after Arles' last bishop. Down this street we can see a magnificent door marking the entrance to the old Hôtel-Dieu. Built in 1587 by Antoine Pons, its classicising vocabulary is typical of Renaissance Arles: fluted columns support an entablature with a carved frieze and a pediment above which there is an inscription commemorating the edifice's construction.

At the corner of the Rue de la République and the Rue Tour-du-Fabre we can note the substantial building that is the Hôtel Laurent de Beaujeu, named after a family of doctors which had other branches in Avignon and Uzès. The ground floor has been changed by the installation of shops, but the three other levels still have their original eighteenth-century structure and decoration, notably the carved lambrequins under the window aprons. We now continue down the Rue de la République to the Hôtel Icard-Duquesne.

Hôtel Icard-Duquesne

19, Rue de la République

THE Icard-Duquesnes, a local family that distinguished itself in the wars at the end of the sixteenth century, occupied this townhouse from the seventeenth century onwards. The building was extensively renovated in the middle of the following

1

2

3

1. Nouvelles Galeries.
2. et 3. Decorative stone faces from the facade of the Hôtel Perrin de Jonquières.

century. It is a fine example of late Louis XV architecture in Arles. The broad three-storey classical facade has large rectangular windows with perfectly judged architraves. But the main distinguishing feature of its decoration is the quality of the ironwork balconies ornamenting its French windows. They remind us of the remarkable levels of skill attained by the master ironworkers of Arles, and indeed of Provence as a whole. O.C.

The building next to the Hôtel Icard-Duquesne is the Hôtel Perrin de Jonquières.

Hôtel Perrin de Jonquières

17, Rue de la République

THIS WELL-PRESERVED and attractively decorated townhouse reflects the wealth and status of the Perrin de Jonquières family, and also their concern with making an impression. Like many other noble families in Arles, their fortune was built on their extensive properties in the Camargue. The townhouse, which can no doubt be dated to the early eighteenth century, has three storeys. Its various decorative styles are noteworthy for the magnificent faces adorning the windows on the first storey, the garlands of flowers and leaves on the second storey windows and the friezes of leaves just beneath the roof, above each window. O.C.

At the end of the Rue de la République we come to the Rue Gambetta, which links the Boulevard des Lices to the Trinquetaille Bridge across the Rhône. This street was laid in 1888, at a time when the avenues of Arles were being widened in order to improve circulation. Cutting through the old medieval town, this new thoroughfare prompted property developers to put up new buildings for rent or stick nineteenth-century facades over older buildings in order to create a perfect alignment. Note at the corner of the Rue de la République and Rue Gambetta, the old Nouvelles Galeries building (now occupied by several different shops), which was built in the early twentieth century after the model of the Parisian department stores. Opposite, on a building occupying the corner of the Rue Gambetta and Rue des Porcelets, a partially erased inscription informs us that this was the location of the shop run by the parents of Jeanne Calment, who lived to the age of 126 and thus became the world's oldest living person (she could remember serving Van Gogh). Here stood the imposing Hôtel des Porcelets, named after a prominent family that governed the La Roquette quarter in the Middle Ages. The Rue des Porcelets specialises in quality food shops and small restaurants. This lively street takes us into the La Roquette quarter, formerly known as the Vieux-Bourg. Until the eighteenth century, when it was united with the Cité quarter, this area was separated by a protective wall.

1

2

1. Quai de la Roquette.
2. L'Œuvre du bouillon.

La Roquette quarter

THE URBAN fabric of this quarter is most unusual: a host of smaller streets branch off from the central thoroughfare, Rue de la Roquette, at an angle. Like fish bones. These streets are now gradually being restored under the conservation regulations governing the whole of the historic centre (54 hectares). It is worth taking the time to wander round here and have a look at the houses for the countless interesting details of their facades: the street-corner recesses, the sculpted doorknockers and masks, etc. This part of the town boasts three churches (Sainte-Croix, Saint-Laurent and Saint-Césaire), a seventeenth-century salt storehouse and some important aristocratic townhouses, making it all in all a very interesting part of Arles to explore.

THE LA ROQUETTE QUARTER used to be dominated by seagoing types, river sailors, ship's captains, fishermen and dockers who worked in the port. This was before the considerable fall in activity along the Rhône as a result of the coming of the railway in 1850. But this now bustling shopping area was also home to many craftsmen and smallholders who contributed to its lively, working atmosphere. Still, the La Roquette quarter was no demotic ghetto, either, as can be seen from the number of large mansions that were built here. O.C.

In the middle of the Rue des Porcelets, turning right into the Rue Georges-Blanc, we can see the renovated facade of the Œuvre du Bouillon at 6, Rue Giraud. In the seventeenth and eighteenth centuries, rich families made numerous donations and bequests to the sick and the needy. At the turn of the eighteenth century, a benefactress by the name of Marie Besson, at the head of a considerable fortune, decided to set up a kind of soup kitchen (*bouillon* means soup or stock) and to operate it from this building, which she adapted to her purpose. The construction has now been converted into flats but still has its old staircase, French ceilings and fireplaces.

Back in the Rue des Porcelets, we now walk on to the Place Paul-Doumer.

Place Paul-Doumer

THIS SQUARE used to be occupied by the Grande Poissonnerie, a fish market that was rebuilt by the Consuls in the eighteenth century. The building was begun by the architect Antoine II Guibert and completed by J. Imbert in 1728. Its form was circular and the framework rested on an entablature of ten Doric columns standing in front of a rectangular hall.

IN 1888, it was replaced by a hall with a large glass ceiling and cast iron superstructure. This was in turn destroyed in 1934. Consequently the farmers' market now put on in this square (except Wednesdays and Saturdays, when there is a big market on the Boulevard des Lices and Boulevard émile-Combes) is held in the open air. O.C.

On the left, looking down the Rue de Chartrouse, we have a clear view of the old church of Sainte-Croix.

1

2

1. Église Sainte- Croix.
2. Église Saint- Laurent.
3. Hôtel de Divonne.
4. Hôtel de Vinsargues.

Église Sainte-Croix

Rue de Chartrouse

IN THE Vieux-Bourg, the parish of Sainte-Croix occupied a larger tract of land than the parish of Saint-Laurent. Its modest inhabitants included agricultural labourers and fishermen. Sainte-Croix is thought to have inherited from the monastery of the Apostles, founded in 547 by Bishop Aurelianus. It housed the tomb of St Florentine, the monastery's first abbot.
MENTIONED as far back as the twelfth century, the church looked very different from what we can see today, which are the vestiges from the reconstruction of 1720. Nationalised and then sold off during the Revolution, it was then further transformed, making it difficult to judge its earlier appearance. All that remains is the upper part of the facade and the bell-tower, the latter housing a bell and a clock mechanism overlooked by the destructive zeal of the Revolution. On the facade, which has been totally deformed by the installation of commercial premises and housing, we can still see one or two elements of its rather Mannerist architecture. As regards the decoration, we can observe the central recess framed by spiral scrolls and surmounted by a tall window and triangular pediment with a round window. M.B.

Crossing the handsome Place Joseph-Patrat, shaded by old plane trees and abutted by the southern side of the church, we come to the Hôtel de Chartrouse.

Hôtel de Chartrouse

31, Rue de Chartrouse

THIS LARGE townhouse, which is now municipal property, was built in around 1820 by the mayor of Arles, the Baron de Chartrouse. It symbolises the social ascension of this figure who was knighted by Napoleon and to whom the people of Arles are indebted for razing the housing that cluttered up the amphitheatre and Roman theatre. His townhouse stands on a sizeable plot of land and has a large garden. The three-storey left-hand building is in a rather severe neoclassical style, but this strictness is attenuated by the ground-floor French windows opening onto the garden, which humanise the ensemble. Inside the building, the salons, staircase and bedrooms have preserved their original dimensions and decoration. O.C.

We now come back to the Place Paul-Doumer, crossing it on the left to reach the Rue Laurent-Bonnemant, where we can see the church of Saint-Laurent on the right.

Église Saint-Laurent

Rue Laurent-Bonnemant

LOCATED in the Bourg-Vieux (the La Roquette quarter), the church of Saint-Laurent still has its Romanesque apse, although it has been drowned out by later constructions. The church was regularly modified and probably rebuilt in 1343. The contract for its belfry, made in 1426, indicates that it had already absorbed the neighbouring church of

3

4

Saint-André. The buildings were reconstructed in 1604. The facade has been thoroughly disfigured, but inside the structure is still clearly visible, with its seventeenth century late Gothic-style nave and several older chapels (fourteenth and fifteenth centuries). The painting for the high altar (now at Saint-Césaire) represents the *Martyrdom of St Lawrence* (1638), by the local painter Trophime Bigot.

UNDER the Ancien Régime, Saint-Laurent was the parish church of a fishermen and sailors' quarter that stretched along the Rhône. This was where the Confraternity of Gardians established their headquarters under the patronage of St George. When the church was deconsecrated, this was transferred to Notre-Dame-de-la-Major. During the Revolution the church was appropriated then sold off by the State, and became a warehouse. Not so long ago it was used as a cinema. M.B.

From the place Paul-Doumer we now take the Rue de la Roquette. At the beginning of the street, on the right, is the Hôtel de Divonne.

Hôtel de Divonne *also known as the* Hôtel du Roure

6, Rue de la Roquette

THIS TOWNHOUSE was almost entirely rebuilt during the eighteenth century by the Du Roures, one of the most illustrious noble families of Arles. This is the only townhouse in Arles to have kept its original plot, including its street-side courtyard and garden at the back. Built after the Parisian model, this edifice has preserved all its original and highly refined ornamentation, as well as most of its internal structure. From the street we can admire its porch complete with the coat of arms of the Du Roure family, the three wings surrounding the courtyard, the grooved decoration of the ground floor and the elegance of the large windows.

THIS TOWNHOUSE was bought by the Divonne family at the beginning of the twentieth century. It has now been divided up into flats. O.C.

We continue down the Rue de la Roquette, passing on our left the Hôtel de Vinsargues (number 15) whose fine restored early seventeenth-century door can be admired in the Rue Parade. Then, on the right, we see the severe-looking Hôtel d'Antonelle (30, Rue de la Roquette), much modified in keeping with its successive functions (once a hospice, and now flats). It does, however, have a charming courtyard. It belonged to the Marquis d'Antonelle, who became the first mayor of Arles in 1791. The Rue Saint-Césaire leads to the church of the same name.

1. Église Saint-Césaire.

Église Saint-Césaire

Rue Rives

FORMERLY the church of the Grands-Augustins convent, it was built in the mid-fifteenth century in the Southern Gothic style and extended in 1492 and 1511. The facade was modified in the nineteenth century. To the sides are distinct traces of two bays that were destroyed by fire in the early seventeenth century. Near the church, protected by railings, are remains of the Grands-Augustins cloister. Inside, the building comprises a nave with four ribbed vault bays flanked by side chapels. The choir, which was transformed in the early nineteenth century, has an octagonal dome with a lantern turret (seventeenth century). In the nave, note the tombs of Honoré de Quiqueran, a Grand Prior of the Order of Malta in the seventeenth century, and Sister Isabellet, the "little saint of La Roquette", who died in 1826. The church has acquired furniture from two other neighbourhood churches, Saint-Laurent and Sainte-Croix. These served parishes with a large seagoing population, which explains the themes of some of the artworks. At the back of the choir is a painting of the *Martyrdom of St Lawrence* made by Trophime Bigot for the high altar of Saint-Laurent in 1638.

SAINT-CÉSAIRE was sold off by the State during the Revolution then acquired by the municipality in 1839 and reinstated as a parish church, now dedicated to St Caesarius, bishop of Arles from 500 to 543. M.B.

Retracing our steps as far as the Rue Sénébier, we now make our way to the banks of the Rhône. This is the heart of the quarter. Walking along the river bank, we come on the left to the Théâtre de la Calade, which was formerly a salt storehouse.

Grenier à sel

49, Quai de la Roquette

OVERLOOKING the Rhône this large and very plain stone building with its two storeys and round arch opening onto the river was built in the seventeenth century to store salt brought in by boat from the Camargue, and later sold further afield in France. The warehouse's position in the port was a functional one. Salt was a rare and therefore costly commodity, subject to a swingeing tax ("la gabelle"). There was another salt storehouse on the opposite bank of the Rhône. As we can see, this one has been converted into a theatre. O.C.

The Rue Rousseau leads us back to the Rue de la Roquette. At the end of this street, on the right, stands the Hôtel Icard-Pérignan.

Hôtel Icard-Pérignan

46, rue de la Roquette

THE ICARD-PÉRIGNANS were a branch of the Icard family. They were solidly established in the La Roquette quarter, where they lived until the Revolution. In the mid-seventeenth century

1. Decoration from the facade of the Hôtel Icard-Pérignan.
2. Église des Carmes-Déchaussés.
3. Tour de l'Écorchoir.

"le sieur d'Icard" built this imposing townhouse, which is now divided up into houses and flats. The refined and unusual decoration chosen for the facade gives a good idea of Icard's wealth. The originality of the ornamentation is most visible on the framing of the windows, with their moulded string courses decorated with spiral scrolls along with fantastic animals, strange faces and foliage. O.C.

We now proceed along the Rue Raillon to the Boulevard Clemenceau, which we cross. The curious facade facing onto the expressway here belongs to the old church of the Discalced Carmelites.

Église des Carmes-Déchaussés

Boulevard de Craponne

IN ARLES, the great Carmelite convent was established in the Cité quarter –very close to today's Place de la République– during the thirteenth century. Come the Revolution it was dismantled and almost completely destroyed. All that remains are a few vestiges in neighbouring houses. The Discalced Carmelites, who came from the same monastic order, as reformed by St Teresa of Avila, came to Arles in 1647. Initially housed by a rich burgher, François Seytour, they began building their own convent in the southern part of the city in 1649. The first stone of the church was laid in 1673 and construction of the monastery buildings was completed in 1678.

IN ADDITION to the church, of which only the facade can still be seen today, these included convent buildings and cloisters. This complex was dismantled during the Revolution. As for the facade of the church, in spite of its poor condition we can still make out the classical style. It is divided vertically into five sections by pilasters with projections. The decoration that stood above the round arched door was destroyed, and the recesses in the two flanking panels are now empty. Two thirds of the way up the facade there is a large entablature dividing it in two. The ensemble was capped by a pediment of which only a few stones remain. O.C.

Going back along Boulevard Clemenceau towards the Rhône, below the expressway, we come to a tower, the Tour de l'écorchoir.

Tour de l'Écorchoir

THE TOUR de l'Écorchoir, in the southwestern part of the La Roquette quarter, is one of the last remaining vestiges of the medieval ramparts along the Rhône. Built in stone, and originally crenellated, it is 16 metres high and has an outer staircase leading to the rampart walk.
IN 1368 Arles was besieged by Bertrand Duguesclin. Four years later, in an effort to strengthen its defences, the town built this protective wall, which at the time had room for several dozen soldiers. Originally it was called the Torre des Leonet, after the name of the owner of the house on which it had been built, Esteve Leon.

Model of the Roman circus.

In 1424, after completion of urgent new work intended to meet the threat from the Aragonese, who had just taken Marseille, the tower was renamed Torre Nova. It was also called Torre Sancta Clara because of its proximity to the port of the same name. In 1431, when Arles was attacked by Catalonian galleys that had sailed up the Rhône, the tower's garrison played an active part in defending the city. And during the civil wars of the late sixteenth century it was used as a watchtower within signalling distance of the Fort de Pâques further downriver, and as an artillery platform from which to meet the enemy fire from the Duc d'Epernon's troops, who were stationed on the opposite bank, at Trinquetaille. In those days Arles was in the hands of the Holy League, an association of militant French Catholics headed by the Duc de Guise who were in conflict with the monarchy.

By the eighteenth century the tower had lost its military importance and was being used as the municipal slaughterhouse. This explains its name, "Tour de l'Écorchoir" (an "écorchoir" being where flaying is done), as well the alternative handle (yet another one), "Tour de la Boucherie". In 1758, at the request of the boatmen, a *bigue* (a post for displaying signals) was raised on the tower so that it could signal the arrival of lighters and allèges. The tower was recently restored. P.R.

Having crossed the Boulevard Clemenceau and passed under the expressway bridge, the imposing blue building of the Musée de l'Arles Antique rises up before us on the right, facing the remains of the Roman Circus.

The Roman circus

Facing the Musée de l'Arles Antique

Ancient circuses (or hippodromes) were built for chariot races and hunting. The one at Arles was 450 metres long and 101 metres wide. It comprised an arena with a packed-earth floor and tiered seating for 25,000 spectators, plus a central division, the *spina,* which is where the obelisk that now stands outside the Hôtel de Ville was positioned. Building work on the Circus began in the year 149 and cannot have been easy, since the instability of the ground required foundations made of thousands of wooden piles as well as regularly placed buttresses. The competitions held here would involve twelve chariot teams who executed seven laps of the track. A visual device made up of stone eggs and bronze dolphins indicated the number of laps left to run. In the sixth century people began quarrying the circus for building material and nowadays there is virtually nothing left. What can be seen, down below the esplanade of the Musée de l'Arles Antique, corresponds to the curving part of the structure, or bend (*the spendone*). Here we can see the substructions of the *cavea* (the tiered seating area). The structure of the circus was similar to that of the amphitheatre, comprising a series of chambers closed by rampant vaults which facilitated movement and held up the seating. C.S.

Musée de l'Arles Antique

Presqu'île du Cirque-Romain

Tel. 04.90.18.88.88

Fax 04.90.18.88.93

Open

March - October: 9.00-19.

November-February: 10.00-17.00

Portrait of a young man.

Ever since the sixteenth century, enlightened townspeople and public authorities have been gathering, collecting and sometimes even producing publications about the vestiges found in the city. The most impressive collection was the one that was exhibited by the Consuls in the vestibule of the town hall from 1614. It included a statue of *Jupiter*, a *Torso of Mithra*, the *Altar of the Good Goddess* and *Medea about to Slaughter Her Children*. All were purchased immediately after discovery.

In 1651, a *Venus* unearthed in the theatre become the jewel of this collection. Unfortunately, it also appealed to Louis XIV, who persuaded the city to "donate" this masterpiece for the park at Versailles.

During the same period, the ecclesiastical authorities were all competing with one other in their zeal to protect their "precious remains". Thus the archbishops' palace and the Dominican monastery were decorated with sculptures, while the Sisters of Mercy (Réligieuses de la Miséricorde) opened a public "garden of antiquities" containing a selection of marble pieces from the Roman Theatre, including *Silenus* figures and *Dancers*, altars and fragments of cornice.

The first museum of antiquities

The first museum in the modern sense of the word was founded in the late eighteenth century by the Minims on the Alyscamps. An agreement dated 7 December 1784 authorised these friars to "gather and assemble in a single place the various ancient monuments found scattered around the town or on its land [...] and to provide easy access for the curious to come and observe them." Unfortunately, the Minims' house was pillaged in 1793 and many works of art were damaged

beyond repair. Nor was this the last of the collections' tribulations. In 1801, the Prefect Delacroix made efforts to get his hands of the treasures so that he could exhibit them in Marseille. Then a political decision was made to have the finest pieces transferred to the Louvre. Pierre Véran, the first keeper of Arles' collection of antiquities, had to use all his skill and diplomacy to resist the pressure. In the end, by an imperial decree dated 9 January 1805, the church of Sainte-Anne was chosen to house the city's ancient heritage and the pieces saved from those turbulent years were duly installed there.

OVER the years the collection grew considerably. By 1935, given the lack of space, it was decided that the Christian artefacts should be moved to the old Jesuit college church.

WHEN the same problem arose again in 1954, the response was to limit the exhibits to statuary from the imperial epoch. This dramatic impoverishment of the displays not only undermined the archaeological coherence of the ensemble, but it also failed to provide a solution to the problem of exhibiting new acquisitions. It was becoming clear that only the construction of a sufficiently capacious museum with an adequate scientific infrastructure would meet the expectations of visitors and researchers while allowing for the collections to be presented cohesively.

The new Musée de l'Arles Antique and its collections

IN THE END, the principle agreed upon was that the new building should be architecturally innovative, a place with a strong identity capable of entering into a dialogue with the ancient masterpieces within. As a result of a nation-wide competition organised by the City of Arles, the project was awarded to Henri Ciriani, and a site was chosen near the Roman circus, which was then being excavated. The triangular plan of the building is articulated in three large sections: a space for the presentation of the permanent collections; a cultural wing with an auditorium and a library; and a scientific wing dedicated to archaeological research, restoration (mosaics and ceramics) and storage.

THE EXHIBITION plan traces the history of Arles from the Neolithic age (no earlier traces of human habitation have as yet been discovered) to the end of Late Antiquity. The presentation is chronological and thematic.

PREHISTORY is prominently represented by the spectacular furniture found in the covered alleys of Le Castelet while the proto-historical period is conveyed by the evocation of three key sites: the sanctuary of Mouriès, L'Arcoule and Arles' Winter Garden, which give an idea of life in the town during the Greek era.

THE BIRTH and development of the Roman town are didactically presented

in exhibits on the Augustan monuments (the Theatre and Forum, those two great vehicles of Augustan propaganda) and later constructions such as the Amphitheatre and the Circus. Plans and models are shown alongside with objects found during excavation work.

THE NEXT set of displays uses stelae and portraits to evoke the army and Roman influence on Arles society. Then pottery glasses and bronze hollowware, all of remarkable quality, offer an idea of domestic life, trade and the crafts. Ingots of copper, pewter and lead bear witness to the trade in raw materials. Various agricultural and crafts activities are illustrated on the sarcophagi known as "l'olivaison" (the olive harvest), "la chasse" (the hunt) and "le bon pasteur" (the good shepherd). The skill of Roman engineers is brought to our attention by a remarkable collection of lead pipes and by models of the Barbegal aqueducts and mills.

Roman mosaic.

STATUES, altars and stelae of gods (Minerva, Cybele, Mithra, Isis) and sculptures of mythological figures (Niobides, Medea, and a remarkable bronze faun) reflect the different cults practised in the city over the years.

THERE IS a whole section devoted to pavements, mainly mosaics, one of which has a central medallion with a very rare illustration of Aeon, the figure used to personify a given epoch. A raised walkway allows visitors to admire these "stone carpets" from a suitable distance.

THE PASSAGE leading to the exit is lined with sarcophagi, which conjure up images of the Alyscamps. These superb marble tombs built for pagans and Christians alike reflect the wealth of Arles' society from the second to the fifth century AD. On the walls, stelae, funerary inscriptions and the fronts of sarcophagi also set us thinking about these inhabitants of ancient Arles whose beliefs and lives are so vividly represented here. C.S.

Around Arles...

1 
2 
3 
 4

1. Joseph-Imbert hospital complex.
2. Chapelle de la Genouillade.
3. French Rail workshops.
4. The Bridge by Van Gogh, 1888 (Otterlo Museum).
Facing page: Abbaye de Montmajour.

Arles' cultural heritage is not restricted to the city as such. Visitors will find the same spirit "outside the city walls" and in the surrounding area. Arles, then, is much more than the immediate city area; it is also a nature park extending from the Alpilles to the Camargue.

JUST OUTSIDE THE CITY

The outlying districts include a number of sites with their own special significance. Naturally these include the sixteenth-century Chapelle de la Genouillade and the "re-created" Van Gogh Bridge, but there are also other, less obviously "historic" sites that add to the interest and charm of the area. A perfect example is the French Rail workshops on the Boulevard Victor-Hugo. Built between 1843 and 1856 and covering in all 11 hectares, they are a fine example of nineteenth-century industrial architecture. Nor are contemporary building approaches absent, as the Joseph-Imbert hospital complex –in the Fourchon district, three kilometres from the city centre– testifies. Designed by Paul Nelson in 1974 it represents a subtle combination of elegance and functionality.

Chapelle de la Genouillade

Route de Crau

THIS SIXTEENTH-CENTURY chapel was part of the Alyscamps necropolis which, in former times, covered several hectares. It was also known as the "Farmers' Chapel", the local brotherhood of farmers having its headquarters there and organising a procession every May. THIS IS a curious-looking structure, with its lowered roof, nineteenth-century steeple and original porch. Framed with pilasters, the main door is surmounted by an entablature and a semicircular pediment with candelabra on each side. The name, etymologically linked to the French word for "knee", refers to a local legend: when Christ came to bless Les Alyscamps, he knelt on a rock on which he left the imprint of his knee. O.C.

Pont Van Gogh

Arles, south of the Barriol district

THE ORIGINAL bridge, made famous by the Van Gogh painting of 1888, was in fact closer to the centre of the city, being situated at Bouc, on the Arles canal. It was demolished during the 1930s and replaced by a concrete version, which in turn was destroyed during the bombings of 1944. The bridge we see now is identical to the one in the painting and was brought here from Fos-sur-Mer in 1960. It has been totally restored and is in perfect working order. O.C.

1

2

1. Aqueduct in the Vallon des Arcs.
2. Countryside near Fontvieille.

IN THE ARLES AREA

The area within a fifty-kilometre radius of Arles offers a host of interesting historical sites, from Montmajour at the foot of the Alpilles to Les Saintes-Maries-de-la-Mer, a village that gives the impression of having grown spontaneously out of the Camargue landscape.

The Fontvieille district

ABOUT seven kilometres from Arles, a little way beyond the Abbaye de Montmajour, Fontvieille and its environs possess an extraordinary cultural richness together with an enormous range of curiosities. This charming setting of hills and low plateaux is home to the entire gamut of Provençal plant life.

Plateau du Castelet

CONTINUING on after the Abbaye de Montmajour, we come to the Plateau du Castelet. Unfortunately the many remarkable prehistoric sites here are not yet open to the public. They all date from the chalcolithic period (2500-1800 BC). The most characteristic contain avenues of standing stones which in all likelihood mark out burial areas.

Vallon des Arcs

THE ROMAN mill known as the Meunerie de Barbegal can be approached from the Mas du Castelet along the D82 road, or from Fontvieille along the D33, locally called the Montée des Pins. Even experienced travellers are unlikely to have visited many places as singular as this one.
EVERY ROMAN town was supposed to have its own water supply and Arles was no exception. A first aqueduct, dating perhaps from Augustan times, brought water from the southern slope of the Alpilles, while a second collected runoff from the north and west slopes. The two met on the hillside facing the village of Fontvieille and from there a single aqueduct carried the water to Arles. Later, perhaps during the reign of Hadrian (117-138 AD), a new aqueduct was added to the southern part of the system: crossing the Vallon des Arcs alongside the aqueduct leading to Arles, it fed a hillside mill that remains the best surviving example of its kind in the Western world.

Early Fontvieille

REGRETTABLY few details are available concerning Fontvieille up until the tenth century, when the two Benedictine abbeys were built. Montmajour remains the better known of the two, but too often at the expense of the Abbaye Saint-Victor-de-Marseille. The local monks set about building the first chapels in the area, that of Saint-Victor (two kilometres from the village, to the left of the D17 road from Arles) and that of Saint-Jean-du-Grès. Recently restored, the latter dates from the eleventh century and is a very fine example of early Romanesque; the reinforcements were doubtless added in the fifteenth or sixteenth centuries.
TO GET TO the Chapelle Saint-Jean-du-Grès, north of the modern village, take the D82, ask for the key at the farm, take the road leading to the cemetery, turn right and then left immediately afterwards. Note the olive trees beside the chapel: the making of olive oil quickly became a major aspect of local farming.

Abbaye de Montmajour

Route de Fontvieille

Tel./fax 04.90.54.64.17

Open all year round

1 October-31 March, 10:00-13:00 and 14:00-17:00

1 April-30 September, 9:00-19:00

Closed on 1 January, 1 May, 1 November, 11 November and 25 December

The Abbaye comprises two groups of buildings created between the eleventh and thirteenth centuries –a handsome tribute to eight centuries of monastic life in the Rhône river area of Provence.

Founded in 949 on an island encircled by marshland, the abbey was home to Benedictine monks who devoted most of their time to prayer, reading, meditation and manual work. By the late thirteenth century there were some sixty of them in all in an abbey whose prosperity was attributable to its landholdings, priories, seigniorial rights and alms-gathering. The abbey was reformed by the monks of Saint-Maur in 1639, secularised in 1786 and sold off in 1791. The partially destroyed buildings were saved by the City of Arles, which acquired them in 1838. They became a listed historical monument in 1840 and were restored under the Second Empire. Since 1945 the abbey has been state property.

The monasteries of Saint-Pierre and Saint-Maur

VISITORS now enter the abbey via the new reception area designed in 1999. It is probably a good idea to visit the medieval monastery of Saint-Pierre before moving on the more modern Saint-Maur, dating from the eighteenth century.

Abbaye de Montmajour. Below: Bird's-eye view of the abbey in the twelfth century

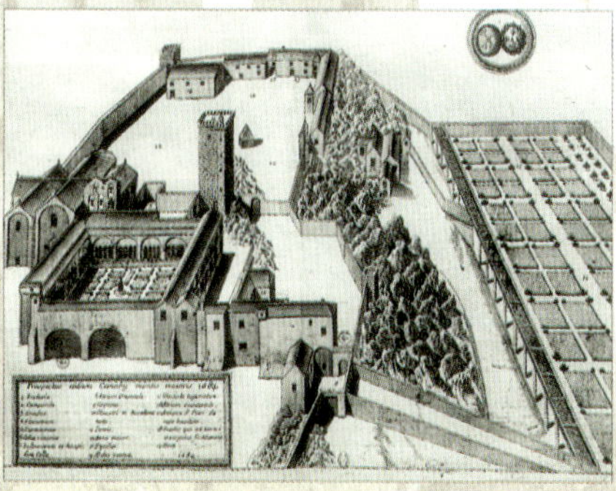

MONASTERY SAINT-PIERRE.
The cloister of the monastery of Saint-Pierre provided a means of communication between all its buildings, of which there remain today only the chapter house, refectory and the remains of the dormitory and the cellar. The beauty of the cloister lies in its architecture and Romanesque decoration. The bell-tower and observation turret (1369) are much higher than the other buildings; at 26 metres the latter offers a splendid view of the surrounding countryside. Built along the north side of the cloister, the twelfth-century abbey church was the liturgical heart of the establishment, the monks coming here for prayer eight times a day. Despite its impressive size and strikingly simple beauty, it was never actually completed. Its round-vaulted choir is decorated with five flat string courses and three unsymmetrically placed windows.

The rib-vault dates from the thirteenth century. The fifteenth century archives hall, the sacristy and the fourteenth-century funerary chapel of Abbé de Maussang, also known as the Chapelle Notre-Dame-de-la-Blanche, adjoin the north side. The crypt beneath the church has a dual function, compensating for the steep fall of the rock, while also serving as an auxiliary church. Its design –a central rotunda, processional path and radiating chapels– is found nowhere else in Provence and its pillars and vaults are dotted with stonemason's marks. Outside the church, the chevet is surrounded by graves hewn into the rock in the shape of human figures. To the east the twelfth-century Chapelle Sainte-Croix with its cloverleaf design is situated beyond the monastery wall and surrounded by hundreds of tombs; this Romanesque jewel is the absolute image of what one imagines a reliquary to be.

Top: Cloister at Montmajour. Middle: Chapelle Sainte-Croix. Above: Walks in the cloister.

Downhill to the east from the Montmajour outcrop is the Ermitage Saint-Pierre, one of whose two chapels was originally a cave. The capitals in the south chapel are decorated with plant and geometrical patterns.

MONASTÈRE SAINT-MAUR.

Moving back uphill towards the tower, we follow the rampart until we gain a view of the gatehouse and the Monastère Saint-Maur from the south terrace. Begun in 1703 this monastery, the work of Avignon architect Pierre Mignard (1640-1725), became the new residence of the Saint-Maur community in 1717. The monks, whose mother-house was the monastery of Saint-Germain-des-Près in Paris, opted for a palatial building inspired by the imposingly functional secular architecture of the time. Of the twenty-eight windows on its northern facade, only four have survived. In 1791 the building was sold and turned into a stonemason's workshop. It became a listed historical monument in 1921 and is currently undergoing detailed restoration with a view to soon being opened to the public.

A.B.

Heritage and photography

MONTMAJOUR is the venue for a special kind of relationship between heritage and photography. As part of the cultural policy of the City of Arles – "Capital City of Photography" – the abbey is closely associated with the annual Rencontres Photographiques d'Arles and the École Nationale de la Photographie.

GIVEN this specific context, the aim is also to utilise photography within the abbey itself: as a means of explaining its history and architecture while making it a living part of the cultural and artistic heritage of the area as a whole. It is further intended to make it into an exhibition centre for national photography collections.

A.M

1. The Daudet mill.
2. Rooftops, Fontvieille.

1

2

Fontvieille, in the shadow of the Tour des Abbés

Despite the existence of other religious centres now extremely isolated or totally inaccessible –among them the Prieuré d'Entremont and the Seigneurie de Mont-Paon, between Fontvieille and Les Baux– Montmajour quickly became a focal point of village life. This was due to the excellent drinking water from its fountain and the presence of the tower known as the Tour des Abbés, which afforded safety from the roving extortionists of the time. Fontvieille really began to expand, however, with the draining of the marshes in the seventeenth century. The creation of the main drainage canal, Le Vigueirat, gave rise to a major local industry –the extraction of dressed stone– whose tradition of craftsmanship remains a part of the local scene to this day. The income this generated allowed the village to begin building a new church, the Église Saint-Pierre-ès-Liens, whose oldest part, the bell-tower, dates from the eighteenth century. The finishing touches were added to the facade in the nineteenth century.

Fontvieille and *Letters from My Mill*

The writer Alphonse Daudet first came to Fontvieille in December 1863, staying at the Château de Montauban, and thenceforth spent part of every winter there for thirty years. His descriptions in *Lettres de mon Moulin* (1866-1868) were used to create the Moulin de Daudet ("Daudet's Mill"), opened in 1935. The upper part is a faithful reconstruction of an early nineteenth-century windmill, while below is a veritable Daudet museum. The mill also provides a fine view of the surrounding countryside. J.-L.M.

The Camargue

THE VAST delta created by the alluvium deposited by the rivers Durance and Rhône spreads eastwards from Avignon to Fos-sur-Mer and westwards as far as the gates of Montpellier. Part of the delta, the Camargue lies between the two branches of the Rhône, sharing the territories of Arles and Les Saintes-Maries-de-la-Mer.

WATER is omnipresent here, with local hydro-management schemes ensuring control of levels and preventing over-salinisation of the soil. The building of the sea wall in 1859 put a stop to encroachment by the sea, but the benefits were offset by completion of the Rhône dykes ten years later, the result being a loss of precious silt and fresh water for the delta. It was only in the twentieth century that a proper irrigation system, with canals and pumping stations, was set up.

WITH a judicious balance now established, the Camargue offers a varied landscape of grasslands and étangs (ponds), the Étang de Vaccarès (6000 hectares) representing almost half the total area of the Nature Park. An official conservation zone, the Camargue is nonetheless home to a range of business activities including cattle and horse raising, farming, hunting, salt extraction and reed cutting.

THE CULTIVATED areas are for the most part given over to rice and wheat. The rice-growing cycle begins with preparation of the ground at the end of winter, followed by sowing in late April. The plants are ripe by August and harvesting takes place from mid-September through to October.

AMONG the area's main attractions are

1

1. Reedbeds.
2. Protected bird.

2

its famous herds of bulls and horses. Hardy and robust, the Camargue horse is, of course, the standard mount of the gardians –the local herdsmen– but is also a great favourite for horseriding excursions. The raising of bulls became an industry in its own right in the early twentieth century and there is a considerable demand for animals for Provençal and Spanish-style bullfights.
APART from Salin-de-Giraud, Les Saintes-Maries-de-la-Mer and perhaps a dozen hamlets scattered across its area, the Camargue is divided up into properties called mas ("farms"), most of which are made up of farmland, marshland and pasture. M.-H.S.

Réserve Nationale de Camargue
SNPN (National Society for the Protection of Nature)

La Capelière, 13200 Arles

Tél. 04.90.97.00.97
Fax : 04.90.97.01.44

E-mail : snpn.reserve.de.camargue@wanadoo.fr

CREATED in 1927, the Réserve Nationale de Camargue –the Camargue Nature Park– falls within the municipalities of Arles and Les Saintes-Maries-de-la-Mer. Its 13,117 hectares are a mosaic of ponds, lagoons, sand dunes, beaches and salt-permeated soil covered with alkali-rich saltwort, a plant of the goosefoot family. The result is an extraordinary biodiversity that includes no less than 272 species of birds. The seasons emphasise this diversity, with the park changing from a salt desert in summer to flood plains in winter. This climatic harshness means there is little in the way of permanent flora and fauna, but thousands of species find temporary refuge here at different times of the year. The migratory and semi-sedentary bird population includes tens of thousands of ducks in winter and up to 40,000 flamingoes, while fish are represented by several dozen fresh, salt and brackish water varieties. The higher ground is occupied by wild boar, foxes and rabbits. The greater part of the park is strictly regulated, but three areas are open to the public:
– LA CAPELIÈRE: As the welcome and information centre for the Camargue Nature Park, La Capelière offers exhibitions, a 1.5 kilometre walking track, four lookout points and two observation platforms overlooking the reed marshes of Vaccarès. It is open daily from 1 April to 30 September, and every day except Tuesday from 1 October to 31 March.
– LA DIGUE À LA MER (the sea wall): 20 kilometres of walking and cycle paths are accessible year-round from the La Gacholle carpark.
– SALIN-DE-BADON: the former royal saltworks now provides an excellent introduction to the area, with 3 kilometres of walking paths, three lookouts and an observation platform.

Salin-de-Giraud and Camargue Salt

THE DISTINCTIVE thing about Camargue soil is its high salt content, but fortunately the terrain –flat, clayey and dotted with ponds– lends itself particularly well to the extraction process. Salt extraction goes back a long way here, but really began to develop in

1

2

1. Saltworks.
2. Salin-de-Giraud.

the late nineteenth century, taking two main forms: at Salin-de-Giraud it was aimed at industry, while further west, at Aigues-Mortes, it was destined for domestic use. Initially producing between 30,000 and 40,000 tonnes per year, the saltworks at Salin-de-Giraud went through a series of ups and downs before stabilising at an annual average figure of 800,000 tonnes extracted from its 11,000 hectares.

How the salt is obtained

1. Collecting the seawater. – This takes place between March and September, the water being drawn directly from the Gulf of Beauduc by three pumps. In all the saltworks take in 80 million cubic metres.
2. Bringing the water to saturation point. – The seawater must be brought from its normal sodium chloride content of 29 grams per litre to saturation at 260 grams. This is done by running it continuously through specially constructed enclosed ponds that maintain a depth –some 35 centimetres as a rule– appropriate to the optimal evaporation rate. At any given time there are some 35 million cubic metres of seawater circulating in the ponds; before reaching saturation they have travelled close to 50 kilometres. This part of the extraction area is home to an enormous variety of bird life, including flamingoes.
3. Settling the salt. – The salt deposit is obtained by further evaporation of the saturated seawater on specially prepared extraction areas. These cover in all 770 hectares of meticulously levelled ground on which the depth of the water averages only 15 centimetres. The saturated brine that remains after the evaporation process takes on a pinkish tinge due to the presence of micro-organisms specific to these local high-salt conditions.
4. Harvesting the salt. – Harvesting takes place between late August and early October; this allows for maximum evaporation and avoids the problems that would otherwise be caused by the autumn rains. By this time the layer of salt is some 7.5 centimetres thick, which gives an average quantity of 1000 tonnes per hectare. The harvest rate is usually 30 hectares per day. According to climatic conditions during the above period, the actual harvest can vary by a factor of up to 4.

History of the Giraud saltworks

Between the thirteenth and mid-nineteenth centuries the local saltwort was incinerated to produce the soda crystals needed for the manufacture of soap and glass. In 1861 Ernest Solvay developed a process for making soda out of salt, which led in time to the opening of a plant on the Giraud salt marshes by Henri Merle, later to found the Péchiney chemicals firm. The end of the nineteenth century saw the growth of the township of Salin-de-Giraud. The town in fact developed as two distinct districts, reflecting the presence of the Solvay and Péchiney companies.

A high-salt ecosystem

The enormous salt-extraction area is of great environmental and ecological interest. The proliferation of certain types of invertebrates provided more than ample food for birds, the result being nesting by species not found together anywhere else in Europe: flamingoes, avocets, terns and others. Certain zones have been protected or re-created in the interests of preserving the local fauna and flora. A.M.

1

2

1. Camargue bull.
2. Domaine de La Palissade.

Marais du Vigueirat

Route de Port-Saint-Louis
13104 Mas Thibert

Tel. 04.90.98.70.91

Fax 04.90.98.72.54

Visits by appointment

THE VIGUEIRAT marshes cover 1000 hectares and represent the largest single acquisition by the Conservatoire du Littoral en Camargue, a conservation body charged with protecting the natural features of the coastline and the lakeshores.

THE REMARKABLE biodiversity of these marshlands is the result of a singular geographical situation produced by the meeting of the two distinctive ecosystems of the Camargue and the Crau. This explains why many animal and vegetable species from both are found together here. The area is a mosaic of humid, biologically diverse Mediterranean habitats in which bulls and horses graze freely –a very special heritage that allows for combining exploration with environmental protection. Guided tours offer a 4-kilometre itinerary through the heart of the marshland.

Domaine de La Palissade

Managed by a semipublic compagny

B.P. 5 – 13129 Salin-de-Giraud

Tel. 04.42.86.81.28

Fax 04.42.48.82.18

Open daily 9:00-17:00
(except public holidays)

THE DOMAINE de La Palissade is one of the last parts of the Camargue to bear witness to the area's age-old struggle between river and sea, soil and salt, water and wind. Visiting the domaine's 702 hectares in summer you find yourself going from desert-like dry areas covered with saltwort to rich reedbeds or forest.

HERE a setting characterised by incredible biodiversity can be explored on foot or on horseback. Set opposite the sea at the mouth of the Grand Rhône, the Domaine de La Palissade is a favourite stopover for migrating birds –notably the thousands of ducks who come for its water plants in winter– while the lagoons fed by the Rhône teem with endless varieties of fish.

FORMERLY a hunting area and horse ranch, the Domaine is now both a splendid introduction to the life and landscapes of the Lower Camargue and a major conservation site. The most significant contributing factor here was its acquisition by the *Conservatoire du Littoral* (see above) in 1997, when there was a very real risk of its being transformed into a housing area. G.D.

Musée Camarguais

Mas du Pont-de-Rousty

Route des Saintes-Maries-de-la-Mer

13200 Arles

Tel. 04.90.97.10.82

Open every day from 1 April to 30 September.
9.15 -17.45 (April, May, Sept..),
9.15 -18.45 (July, August).
Open every day except Tuesdays from 1 Oct. to 31 March,
10.15-16.45
Closed 1 Jan., 1 May and 25 Dec.

In 1973 the foundation in charge of the Camargue Nature Park acquired part of the buildings and land of the Mas du Pont-de-Rousty, 12 kilometres from Arles. Subsequently it was decided to turn the sheepfold into the Musée Camarguais.

This building is typical of the large-scale sheepfolds that were built in the Camargue in the early nineteenth century, their design being based on that of the traditional reed-thatched cottages found in the area. However the flimsiness of this kind of roof and its vulnerability to fire led sheepfold owners to replace the thatch with flat tiles, as was done at the Pont-de-Rousty farm in about 1945. After its acquisition by the foundation, the building was restored and fitted out and the museum, with its substantial collection of exhibits and documentary material, was opened in 1979. It has been awarded the "European Museum Prize". ITS INTRODUCTION to the Camargue begins with a presentation of the Rhône delta from its geological formation up until the twentieth century. This is followed by an account of its various inhabitants at the major stages in its history. Archaeological remains dating from just prior to its earliest recorded history are complemented by an extensive coverage of the Roman era and the Middle Ages, when devotion to the three "Saint Marys from the Sea" began (these were Mary Magdalen, Mary Jacobi, the sister of the Virgin Mary, and Mary Salome, mother of the apostles James and John). A significant part of the permanent exhibition is given over to traditional nineteenth-century activities –crop and livestock farming, food-gathering, hunting and fishing– and such twentieth-century developments as water control, wine and rice growing, salt extraction, tourism and protection of the environment.

The museum's temporary exhibitions offer visitors a good introduction to the nature park; this is backed up by a 3.5 kilometre walk allowing them to discover a local farm, irrigated and cultivated areas, high-salt areas used as pasture, reedbeds and marshland.
M.-H.S.

1. Les Saintes-Maries-de-la-Mer: the church.
2. Village of Saintes-Maries-de-la-Mer.
3. The Gypsy pilgrimage.

Château d'Avignon

Route des Saintes-Maries-de-la-Mer

DATING from the second half of the 18th century, the château was situated on a vast farming property created in the 1730s by the Arles aristocrat François-Joseph d'Avignon d'Arlatan. By the beginning of the nineteenth century the domain covered 23,000 hectares bordered by the Petit Rhône, the Vaccarès district and the sea. At the end of the century it became the property of Louis Prat and his mother, Anne Rosine Noilly, directors of the Noilly Prat firm in Marseille. They renovated the château –unfortunately in a less sober style– and turned it into a relatively comfortable hunting lodge. In 1989 the Bouches-du-Rhône département acquired it and carried out a much more successful renovation. The grounds offer the visitor an interesting range of plant life.

Saintes-Maries-de-la-Mer

SITUATED at the mouth of the Petit Rhône and surrounded by ponds and lagoons, this is a charming village on the shores of the Mediterranean.

The church

A HOST of local legends and traditions make the church the point of departure for the founding of the village. The building as we know it today, however, is the latest in a succession of places of worship, the first dating –according to tradition– from the fifth or sixth century. At that time the locality was known by the same name –Beata Maria de Ratis– as the shrine that went on to become a place of pilgrimage. Existing records indicate that it was destroyed and rebuilt at the time of the barbarian invasions, with a church appearing on the site of the original chapel between the ninth and twelfth centuries. This church still stands today, but was fortified in the thirteenth and fourteenth centuries by the addition of machicolations and the building of a crenellated keep. Given its strategic military situation, it was also topped with a watchtower. Thus fortified, it doubtless served as a refuge for the people of the village in cases of attack by irregulars or pirates. The architectural style of the building is characterised by an extreme sobriety and internal decoration is limited to two cornices.
THE EX-VOTOS covering the walls of the nave date from the sixteenth to the nineteenth centuries and are fine examples of Provençal folk art. Under the nave is a crypt, entered from outside the church; this is home to the statue of St Sara, the "Black Virgin" venerated by the Gypsies.

The pilgrimage

IN THE FIFTEENTH century Notre-Dame-de-Radeau became Notre-Dame-de-la-Mer. After a number of miraculous cures, notably that of the bishop of Saint-Pol-de-Léon in 1347, the devotion focusing on the church became more intense. An influential legend of the time had it that three saints –Mary Jacobi, Mary Salome and Mary Magdalene– had been driven out of Palestine by the Jews at the time of Christ's crucifixion.
Set adrift in a small boat with neither sails nor oars, the three, accompanied

2

3

by their servant Sara the Egyptian, seemed condemned to certain death; but after many days at sea they were cast up on the shores of the Camargue, where they founded a shrine on the site of what was later Les Saintes-Maries-de-la-Mer and performed a number of miracles.

THIS UPSURGE of piety led King René to authorise excavations in 1447, the aim being to recover the remains of the three holy women. Their bones were found, declared authentic by the Church and given their own shrine as relics.

EVERY YEAR since then, on 25 May and the nearest Sunday to 22 October, pilgrimages are held in honour of the three "Saint Marys from the sea". These events, focusing on a sacred fresh-water well on the site of the present church and the "Invention" or discovery of the relics by King René, continue to generate tremendous fervour. During the ceremony the relics in their containers are brought down from their high chapel into the nave; they are then escorted in procession to the sea to be blessed by the celebrant, surrounded by Camargue herdsmen on horseback and an enormous crowd of the faithful.

SINCE 24 May 1935, the Gypsies also assemble here to pay honour to their patroness Sara, regarded by them as a saint despite being uncanonised by the Church. This custom began in the early twentieth century when some thousand Gypsies from Spain and southern France attended the ceremonies at Les Saintes-Maries-de-la-Mer. In 1935 the Marquis Folco de Baroncelli persuaded the Archbishop of Aix to allow the statue of Sara to be brought out of the crypt and admitted, with the Gypsies, to the Sunday procession. Now large groups of Gypsies come long distances every year to take part in the pilgrimage, which has also become for them an occasion for baptisms and marriage proposals.

The village today

SINCE the Middle Ages the currents produced by climatic changes have considerably modified the Camargue shoreline and gradually eroded the coast near Les Saintes-Maries-de-la-Mer. Originally several kilometres distant, by 1838 –when the village took on its present name– the sea was already only a kilometre away. Today Les Saintes-Maries-de-la-Mer is protected by dykes and breakwaters, without which it would be partially flooded by the sea. What was once no more than a humble fishing village is now a seaside resort in its own right, with a fishing and sailing port, a convention centre, a thalassotherapy establishment and a bullring built in 1937.

Musée Baroncelli

THE BUILDING that houses the Musée Baroncelli and its collections dates from 1876. Designed by Véran in the style of the Third Republic, it served as town hall and law courts before becoming the municipal museum. The collections themselves were assembled in 1942. Presented under a range of subject headings, they are for the most part made up of stuffed animals, archival material, paintings and furniture. J.F.

Local events

Arles, city of art and history

• Guided tours: "The Story of Arles", 1 July – 30 September. For rates and reservations, contact the TOURIST OFFICE.
• Free guided tours of the sights: for times and other information, contact the TOURIST OFFICE.
• Group visits all year round: contact the TOURIST OFFICE.
• Educational services: contact the SERVICE DU PATRIMOINE.

Fête des Gardians (Herdsmen's Festival)

1 May
Information:
TOURIST OFFICE
or FESTIVALS COMMITTEE

This festival is linked to the feast of St George, patron saint of the gardians or Camargue herdsmen, whose brotherhood, founded in 1512, is the oldest in France. The herdsmen assemble on the Boulevard des Lices at nine in the morning, the actual procession beginning with a salute to Frédéric Mistral at 9:30 and the placing of the traditional bouquet at the foot of his statue on the Place du Forum by the "Queen of Arles", chosen every three years on the day of the festival. The procession of a hundred horsemen, accompanied by tambourine players and women

The "Course de Satin"

Mid-June
Information:
TOURIST OFFICE
or FESTIVALS COMMITTEE

The day begins with bull-branding, with the afternoon devoted to tests of horsemanship: manoeuvring, "taiolo", speed and the "Course de Satin" in which the competitors ride bareback. The winner is awarded a satin scarf, but this only becomes his property after three consecutive victories.

Rencontres Internationales de la Photographie

Early July – mid-August
10, Rond-Point des Arènes
Tel. 04.90.96.76.06
Fax 04.90.49.94.39

In 1970, Lucien Clergue, Michel Tournier and Jean-Maurice Rouquette founded the Rencontres Internationales de la Photographie in Arles.
Since then the city has become a significant contributor to the history of photography and the venue for one of France's most prestigious cultural events.

La Pegoulado

The Friday evening preceding the Fête du Costume
Information:
TOURIST OFFICE
or FESTIVALS COMMITTEE

Tourist Office or Festivals Committee La Pegoulado is Arles' most highly symbolic festival. The whole city takes part in this *paso carriero* ("parade"), which closes with an evening in the Arena. Eagerly awaited all year long by the Arlesians, this event really does reveal the soul of the city.

Fête du Costume

First Sunday in July
Théâtre antique
Information:
TOURIST OFFICE
or FESTIVALS COMMITTEE

The Costume Festival was founded in 1903 by Frédéric Mistral, who wanted to make the wearing of traditional dress a symbol, a mark of honour and a public event. For that initial festival eighteen young people answered his call, a figure that house now risen to over a thousand. Here we have tradition raised to the level of art, as the people of Arles turn out in all their finery.

The Cocarde d'Or

The Monday following the Costume Festival
Information:
Tourist Office
or Festivals Committee

First held in 1930, this is the oldest and most respected of the local Provençal bullfight events.

Festival des Suds

Second week of July
BP 147 – 13631 Arles Cedex
Tel. 33 (0)4.90.96.06.27
Fax: 33 (0)4.90.96.79.48
http: //www.suds-arles.com
e-mail: contact@suds-arles.com

Since 1996, Arles has been vibrating to the excitement of this week-long mid-July festival.
The city streets are full of the musical warmth of those southern countries that have already sent us Cesaria Evora, Goran Bregovic, Cheb Mami, I Muvrini, Faudel and many others.
All this plus aperitifs and neighbourhood meals in the street –so come along for a taste!

Féria d'Arles

Easter and the second weekend of September
Information:
Tel. 04.90.96.03.70

A bullfight festival and a host of related events: bulls in the streets, Camargue bullfights in dismountable bullrings, music, concerts, exhibitions, releasing of horses into the Camargue, and the "toro de fuego".
Over the years the Arles Feria has earned itself a place among the country's top bullfight festivals.

Les Prémices du riz

Mid-September
Information:
Tourist Office
or Festivals Committee

Every year Arles celebrates the rice harvest, then in full swing in the Camargue.
The whole city and its surrounding area –neighbourhoods, villages, community associations– is involved in preparing the Corso, the parade of colourful floats through the streets of Arles.
A whole month of celebrations in honour of a tradition, a calling, a rice-growing area and all those who live there.

Salon International des Santonniers

Late November – mid-January
Information:
Tel.: 04.90.96.47.00

First organised in 1958 by Provence's master santon makers and the City of Arles, this fair continues to present the region's traditional Christmas crib figures and their equivalents from around the world.
The works –150 in all, and 80 per cent of them new creations– are shown in the impressive medieval setting of the Saint-Trophime cloister.

Useful addresses

Tourist Office

Boulevard des Lices
13200 Arles
Tel. (33) 04.90.18.41.20
Fax (33) 04.90.18.41.29
www.arles.org
E-mail: ot-arles@visitprovence.com

Service du Patrimoine

HÔTEL DE VILLE (ANNEXE)
5, Rue du Cloître
13200 Arles
Tel. (33) 04.90.49.38.20
Fax (33) 04.90.49.35.30
E-mail: patrimoine@ville-arles.fr

Festivals Committee

35, Place de la République
13200 Arles
Tel. (33) 04.90.96.47.00

Hôtel de ville / Town Hall

Place de la République
BP 196 - 13637 Arles Cedex

Index of streets, sites and monuments

THIS INDEX lists only streets, squares, sites and monuments directly linked to Arles and its environs. The names and page numbers in bold indicate a full article in the book.

PHOTO CREDITS

Archives Municipales, Arles : p. 27 a, 27 b, 28 a, 28 b, 29, 37.
Médiathèque, Arles : p. 63 a, 95.
– photographs Michel Lacanaud : p. 33 a, 34 a.
Musée de l'Arles Antique, Arles : p. 13 b, 15, 69, 73, 74 a, 127 b.
– photographs Yvon Fruneau : p. 8 b, 17, 24, 46 b, 48 b, 50 a, 55 (3), 63 b, 67 a, 68, 78 (2), 85 b, 88 b, 104 a.
– photographs Marc Heller : p. 8 a, 13 a, 113 (3), 124.
– photographs Michel Lacanaud : p. 45 (4), 125, 126, 127 a.
Musée Réattu, Arles : p. 7, 99 a, 99 b, 100, 102 a, 102 b.
– photograph Michel Lacanaud : p. 101.
Museon Arlaten, Arles :
– photograph Michel Lacanaud : p. 113 (2).
– photographs J.-L. Mabit : p. 9 c, 9 d, 67 b, 113 (1), 115 (1), 116 (1), 116 (2), 116 (3).
– photograph R. Wilson : p. 115 (2).
Parc National Régional de Camargue (PNRC) : p. 9 e, 38, 134 (1), 136 (1), 137, 139 (2).
Service du Patrimoine, Arles : p. 8 e, 32, 47 b, 51, 56 (1), 64, 65 a, 74 b, 77 (1), 103, 107 (3), 129 (1), 131 b.
– Yacine Azzoug (drawings): p. 49, 57.
– photographs Andreas Hartmann-Virnich : p. 45 (1), 48 a, 86 b.
– photographs Aldo Bastié : p. 70 (1), 70 (2).
– photographs Françoise Thurel : p. 62 (1), 72, 79 (2), 80 (2), 90 (1), 114, 120 (1), 120 (2), 123 (2).
– photographs Michel Baudat : p. 34 b, 77 (2), 78 (1), 90 (2), 122 (1).
– photographs Henri-Luc Casès : p. 8 c, 53, 58 (2), 59 (4), 59 (5), 60 (1), 60 (2), 62 (2), 66 (1), 71 (3), 71 (5), 105, 108-109 (2), 117 (1), 117 (4), 118 (2), 118 (3), 121 (3).
– photographs Odile Caylux : p. 33 b, 82, 92, 110 (1), 117 (2), 119 (2).
Société Nationale de Protection de la Nature (SNPN) : p. 134 (2).
Ville d'Arles, Service Communication :
– photographs Daniel Bounias, Johann Delacour, Valérie Farine, Hervé Hote, Lionel Roux, Samuel Thomas : p. 1, 2, 5, 8 d, 9 b, 10, 11, 18, 19 a, 19 b, 21, 23 a, 23 b, 30, 31, 39, 40, 41 a, 41 b, 42, 43, 45 (2), 45 (3), 46 a, 47 a, 50 b, 52 (1), 52 (2), 54, 55 (2), 56 (2), 58 (1), 59 (3), 61 (1), 61 (2), 65 (2), 66 (2), 71 (4), 75, 79 (1), 80 (1), 81 (3), 83, 84, 85 a, 86 a, 88 a, 89, 91 (3), 93 (4), 94 (1), 97 (1), 97 (2), 98, 103, 104 b, 106 (1), 106 (2), 107 (4), 108 (1), 109 (3), 110 (2), 111 (3), 115 (bas), 117 (3), 117 (5), 118 (1), 119 (1), 121 (4), 123 (1), 123 (3), 129 (2), 129 (3), 130 a, 130 b, 133 (1), 133 (2), 135 (1), 135 (2), 136 (2), 138 (1), 139 (3).

Published by Editions du patrimoine
General Editor: Dominique Carré.
Assistante Editor: Christine Richet.
Graphic design: Raymonde Branger.
Production manager: Carine Merse.
Photoengraving: Scann'Ouest, Nantes.
Printing: Néo Typo, Besançon.

Printed in june 2001.
Dépôt légal : june 2001.